PROJECT FOR TRANSLATION AND PUBLICATION OF CHINESE CULTURAL WORKS

中国文化著作翻译出版工程项目

CLASSICAL CHINESE POETRY AND PROSE

DREAM IN PEONY PAVILION

TANG XIANZU

TRANSLATED BY XU YUANCHONG & FRANK M. XU

许译中国经典诗文集

牡丹亭

【明】汤显祖 著

许渊冲 许明 译

五洲传播出版社
China Intercontinental Press

中華書局
Zhonghua Book Company

PUBLISHER'S NOTE

Ancient Chinese classic poems are exquisite works of art. As far as 2,000 years ago, Chinese poets composed the beautiful work *Book of Poetry* and *Elegies of the South*. Later, they created more splendid Tang poetry and Song lyrics. Such classic works as *Thus Spoke the Master* and *Laws Divine and Human* were extremely significant in building and shaping the culture of the Chinese nation. These works are both a cultural bond linking the thoughts and affections of Chinese people and an important bridge for Chinese culture and the world.

Mr. Xu Yuanchong has been engaged in translation for 70 years. He won the Lifetime Achievement Award in Translation conferred by the Translators Association of China (TAC) in 2010, and won the "Aurora Borealis" Prize for Outstanding Translation of Fiction Literature, conferred by the Federation of International Translators (FIT) in 2014. He is honored as the only expert who translates Chinese poems into both English and French. After his excellent interpretation, many Chinese classic poems have been further refined into perfect English and French rhymes. This collection of Classical Chinese Poetry and Prose gathers his most representative English translations. It includes the classic works *Thus Spoke the Master*, *Laws Divine and Human* and dramas such as *Romance of the Western Bower*, *Dream in Peony Pavilion*, *Love in Long-life Hall* and *Peach Blooms Painted with Blood*. The largest part of the collection includes the translation of selected poems from different dynasties. The selection includes various types of poetry. The selected works start from the pre-Qin era to the Qing Dynasty, covering almost the entire history of classic poems in China. Reading these works is like tasting "living water from the source" of Chinese culture.

We hope this collection will help English readers "understand, enjoy and delight in" Chinese classic poems, share the intelligence of Confucius and Lao Tzu (the Older Master), share the gracefulness of Tang poems, Song lyrics and classic operas and songs and promote exchanges between Eastern and Western culture. We also sincerely invite precious suggestions from our readers.

出版前言

中国古代经典诗文是中国传统文化的奇葩。早在两千多年以前，中国诗人就写出了美丽的《诗经》和《楚辞》；以后，他们又创造了更加灿烂的唐诗和宋词。《论语》《老子》这样的经典著作，则在塑造、构成中华民族文化精神方面具有极其重要的意义。这些作品既是联接所有中国人思想、情感的文化纽带，也是中国文化走向世界的重要桥梁。

许渊冲先生从事翻译工作70年，2010年荣获“中国翻译文化终身成就奖”，2014年荣获国际译联颁发的“北极光”杰出文学翻译奖。他被称为将中国诗词译成英法韵文的唯一专家，经他的妙手，许多中国经典诗文被译成出色的英文和法文韵语。这套“许译中国经典诗文集”荟萃许先生最具代表性的英文译作，既包括《论语》《老子》这样的经典著作，又包括《西厢记》《牡丹亭》《长生殿》《桃花扇》等戏曲剧本，数量最多的则是历代诗歌选集。这些诗歌选集包括诗、词、散曲等多种体裁，所选作品上起先秦，下至清代，几乎涵盖了中国古典诗歌的整个历史。阅读和了解这些作品，即可尽览中国文化的“源头活水”。

我们希望这套许氏译本能使英语读者对中国经典诗文也“知之，好之，乐之”，能够分享孔子、老子的智慧，分享唐诗、宋词、中国古典戏曲的优美，并以此促进东西文化的交流。也敬请读者朋友提出宝贵意见。

CONTENTS
目　　录

ACT II
第二本

ACT III
第三本

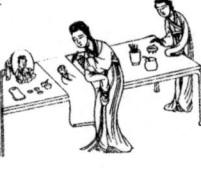

ACT IV
第四本

ACT V
第五本

CLASSICAL CHINESE POETRY AND PROSE

DREAM
IN PEONY PAVILION

TANG XIANZU

TRANSLATED BY XU YUANCHONG & FRANK M. XU

China Intercontinental Press Zhonghua Book Company

PREFACE

There were four classics of poetic drama in Chinese history, that is, *Romance of the Western Bower, Dream in Peony Pavilion, Love in the Long-life Hall* and *Peach Blossom Painted with Blood.* The subject of the *Romance* is the conflict between love and honor of a feudal family, and that of the *Dream* is the life and death of a lover. In the former, love triumphs over honor, and in the latter it further triumphs over death. In the mean time, we have Shakespeare's tragedies in rivalry with Chinese classics in the Western countries, though they are two hundred years later than the *Romance* but earlier than *Long-life Hall* and *Peach Blossom.* In the *Romance,* the lovers are separated by the mother's idea of honor and re-united by the hero's success in the civil service examinations, while in Shakespeare's tragedy, Romeo and Juliet are separated by enmity between their parents but re-united by death. The happy ending of the *Romance* shows the progress of Chinese civilization while the tragic end of *Romeo and Juliet* hints at the conquest of enmity by reason which foretells the triumph of realistic and scientific spirit. Here we can see the different development of Oriental and Occidental civilisation.

The author of the *Dream in Peony Pavilion* was a contemporary of Shakespeare and the *Peony Pavilion* is his representative work while Shakespeare's is *Hamlet.* Can their representative works be compared? *Hamlet* begins with the revival of the dead king who tells his son how he was poisoned by his brother who usurped his throne and married his wife. The son is not sure of the truth of what the dead king said, so we have the well-known monologue in Act III:

To be or not to be that is the question:
Whether 'tis nobler in the mind to suffer
The slings and arrows of outrageous fortune
Or to take arms against a sea of troubles,
And by opposing end them,

Here *to be* may mean to *take arms* and *not to be, to suffer*; the *outrageous fortune* may refer to the murder of his father, his uncle's usurpation of the throne and his mother's re-marriage. He hesitates about what to do: whether he should suffer for the love of his mother or rise to revenge the death of his father. Here we see the conflict in his mind or contradiction in his inner world. Besides, there is conflict in the outer world. For instance, we see the contradiction between uncle and nephew in the following dialogue:

Uncle: *But now, my cousin Hamlet, and my son*
Nephew: *A little more than kin and less than kind!*
Uncle: *How is it that the Clouds still hang on you?*
Nephew: *Not so, my lord. I am too much in the sun.*

The usurper uncle is unwilling, but he cannot refuse, to call his nephew *my son*, nor is the nephew willing to be so called, but he is very clever at reply by playing on the words *kin* and *kind, son* and *sun*, implying that the uncle is not a kind kin, and that it would be too much for himself to have been called *son* by his father and mother, and now by his uncle, who is compared to the clouds that overshadow the sun (son). There is conflict not only between uncle and nephew but also between mother and son, for example, we may read the following dialogue:

Mother: *Hamlet, thou hast thy father much offended.*
Hamlet: *Mother, you have my father much offended.*

Hamlet playing on words has offended his uncle but the mother's second marriage with her husband's brother has offended her first husband. Here we find the contradictions complicated.

In the *Dream of Peony Pavilion* the contradiction is simple. We find more contradictions in the outer world than in the inner one. There are contradictions between the heroine and her father, her mother, and her teacher, more contradictions than in her own mind. For instance, we may read the teacher's song sung to the tune of *Changing Roles* in Scene 2, Act II.

Of the Six Classics the Book of Poetry is true
To life. It shows what a noble lady should do.
The Story of the Lord of Corn
Tells her not to forget by whom she's born.
She should be pious to her mother,
And not be jealous of another,
Be virtuous as a queen
Whenever she is seen.
At cock's crow she should rise,
and grieve when swallow away flies.
...
She would wash powder off her face
And live with grace.
She'd be a faithful wife
And lead a virtuous life.
...
The three hundred poems in the Book of Poetry, in a word teach you to do no wrong.

Does the heroine believe what her teacher says? Read what her maid says in Scene 3, Act II:

When the teacher taught my young mistress the *Book of Poetry*, she sighed at the following verse:

By riverside are cooing
A pair of turtledoves;
A good young man is wooing
A fair maiden he loves.

Closing the book, she said, here we can see the heart of a sage and the feeling shared alike by the ancient and the modern.

That is to say, she may not believe what his teacher tells her, *to lead a virtuous life*. What is more, we may read her own monologue in Scene 4, Act II:

O Heaven! Now I believe spring is stirring the heart. I have read in long or short poems of ancient days that maidens were moved in spring and grieved in autumn. Now I understand the reason why. I'm sixteen years of age, but where is the young man who would win the laureate for me, or fly up to the moon to woo the beauty in the silver palace?

This monologue reveals the contradiction of love and virtue in her heart. When love triumphs over virtue in the end, she feels no contradiction any more. This shows there is more contradiction in the outer world than in the inner world in the *Peony Pavilion*. The play begins with a dream of love, follows by her death for love and ends by her revival and marriage with her lover. It may be called a trilogy of love while Shakespeare's tragedy may be called a trilogy of enmity and death, for it begins with the revival of the dead king for revenge, follows with the performance of the murder on the stage and ends by the death of the hero, his mother and his uncle.

Comparing these two trilogies, we can see the difference

between the Chinese and English dramatic works is one between love and hate (or virtue and revenge), and another between the inner and the outer worlds. As to the characterization, the Chinese characters are simple while the English ones are complicated. As to the language, in Shakespeare, we find more play on words, while in the Chinese play more comparisons are used, for instance:

He leaned on the rock by lakeside,
I stood like a jade statue vivified.
He carried away his jade mate
Who might in warm sunlight evaporate.

In short, they may be compared in four aspects: plot, characterization, situation and language.

Frank M. Xu at OKC. USA.

ACT I

Scene 1 Prelude

(Enter the author Tang Xianzu.)

Tang (Singing to the tune of ***Butterflies in Love with Flowers***):

No longer busy, I live at leisure,
Thinking over where I can find pleasure.
Writing heart-breaking verse by day,
What of love can a lover say?
Sitting in my hall day and night,
The fair scene beautifies my verse
Even in candlelight,
For better or worse,
If you are worthy of her love,
You'd win a new life from above.

(Changing to the tune of ***Spring in Han Palace***):

Governor Du Bao had a daughter fair,
Fond of treading on the green here and there.
She was lovesick of a young scholar she
Dreamed of who'd break for her a twig off a willow tree.
Leaving a portrait, she died,
Buried lonely by mume flowers' side.
After three years,
The scholar dreaming of mume lowers appears
And brings her back to life.
They soon become man and wife.

He takes the court exam at the capital,
For honor first of all.
But rebels rise,
And take Governor Du's town by surprise.
The scholar coming to inquire
Is taken for a liar.
Fortunately the decree comes down:
He has won the laurel crown.

Epilogue of the Story

The fair maiden died, leaving her portrait fair.
Her father freed the town of rebels there.
The Dreamer won the fair coming to life again.
How could he not of unjust punishment complain?

Scene 2 Liu Dreamer of Mume Flower

(Enter Liu Dreamer of Mume Flower.)

Liu (Singing to the tune of ***Pearl Screen***):

Born in a family nobler by far
Than those under a lucky star,
Poor now I still remain,
After cold wind and rain.
'Tis said books will bring wealth, beauty and gold,
I'm disappointed to have in vain grown old.
What can I be
But a man right and free?

(Changing to the tune of ***Partridges in the Sky***):

I study hard till frost
On tortoise's back is lost.
Living from hand to mouth,
A poor scholar loves the south.
Relying on natural gifts better or worse,
I can read and write prose and verse.
Borrowing light and pricking my thigh,
I've learned the art of writing from on high.
I do not know if my arms can cut the tree down,
Till I have won the laurel crown.

I am Liu Dreamer of Mume Flower and Lover of Spring, descendent of Liu Zongyuan, poet of the Tang Dynasty, and resident south of the Five

Ridges. My father was an official and my mother a county lady. (Sighing) Unfortunately they died early and left me an orphan, living a hard life since my childhood. But fortunately I have grown up to twenty and I am intelligent enough to have passed the three examinations. As I hold no office, I earn a living not free from hunger and cold. My ancestor had an expert gardener Hunchback Guo, whose descendent, also a gardener, keeps me company in Guangzhou. This is not the way for a promising young man, so I feel melancholy all day long. Half a month ago, I dreamed of a fair maiden standing under a mume tree, beautiful just to the point, who told me with a winning smile to win her heart and hand, and also win success in my career, so I changed my name to Dreamer of Mume Flower and Lover of Spring.

Dreams long or short are only dreams;
Years in and out pass like her gleams.

(Singing to the tune of ***Innermost Feeling***):

Though I have changed my name,
How could the beauty know my flame?
I wish to wear the laurel crown,
But I cannot boast of my gown.
The jealous Moon Goddess may wither the flower,
I'll wait until my eyebrows knit
And my heart sour
As if drunken I feel unfit.

(Changing to the tune of ***Three Scholars***):

I bore a hole for the fireflies,
For eastern walls allow no peeping eyes.
When spring gilds willow trees,
And snowflakes make mumetiers freeze,

Then through the thoroughfare I'll ride,
And choose the silk whip from my bride.

Well, I have here a friend who is descendent of Han Yu, famous scholar of Tang Dynasty, and I would like to profit from his counsel.

Epilogue of the Scene

Before the door spring shines on mume and willow trees.
How could I dream of royal favor as I please?
Unlike the flower in full bloom my heart appears.
Could I grow green as a pine of ten thousand years?

Scene 3 Parental Admonition

(Enter Du Bao, prefect of Nan'an.)

Du (Singing to the tune of ***Courtyard Full of Fragrance***):

Then scholar of the West,
Now prefect in the south,
I work at court or rest
By riverside or at its mouth.
In crimson robe with golden belt I'm drest,
Who could say I've not done my best?
I won't regret my hair turns gray,
But I'd go home a thousand miles away.
I can't retire, I am afraid,
My home-going steeds are delayed.
"I'm a prefect all my life long.
Don't think I've done anything wrong.
I drink but water from the fountain;
I like to sit and face the mountain."

I am Du Bao, prefect of Nan'an in the south and descendent of Du Fu, famous poet of Tang Dynasty who lived in the west for long. Now I am over fifty years old. Since I passed the civil service examinations at the age of twenty and served as prefect for three years, I have built my reputation as a good prefect. My wife is Lady Zhen, descendent of Empress Zhen of Wei Dynasty, whose family living near Mount Eyebrows is known for its virtue. We have only one daughter, a fair maiden not yet engaged. As a well-educated daughter should be well married, I should like to discuss the matter with my wife now I am unoccupied today.

A daughter may transmit my fame;
Since I've no son to tarnish my name.
(Enter Lady Zhen)

Lady Zhen (Singing to the tune of ***Around the Pool***):

Descendent of Princess Zhen by riverside,
My family did in the west reside.
Having left Mount Eyebrows,
I'm the first Lady of Nan'an now;
(They greet each other.)

Du: I become prefect with no virtue high.

Lady Zhen: I'm the first lady none deny.

Du: What is our daughter doing at her leisure?

Lady Zhen: She is doing her needlework with pleasure.

Du: As for needlework, I think she is good enough. But since old days, fair maidens should be good in reading and writing, so that when she is married to a well-educated scholar, they may keep good company all their life long. What do you think of it, Madame?

Lady Zhen: You are right, my lord.

(Enter Du the Belle followed by her maid Fragrant Spring with a tray of wine cups.)

Belle (Singing to the previous tune):

Even orioles will sing
Of the beauty of spring.
How can young grass repay

The warm light of spring day?

(Greeting her parents) A hundred blessings, dear Dad and Mom.

Du: Why have you brought wine cups here?

Belle (Kneeling): Spring is so fine and you are enjoying your rest in the rear hall. So I come to offer you three cups of wine with my best wishes.

Du (Laughing): You are quite thoughtful.

Belle (Singing to the tune of ***Drunken Jade Mountain***):

A hundred blessings to you!
Your daughter overjoyed in view
Of the rear hall where spring days shine,
Would offer you three cups of wine.
Though I regret to have no brother,
A later son would bring joy to father and mother.

Together: Let's raise our cup!
After a daughter will a son come up.

Du: Fragrant Spring, fill the cup of your young mistress.

(Singing to the previous tune):

Our ancestor Du Fu regretted to roam
With his family far away from home.
Do you not think I'm even worse,
For he had sons to read his verse,
While I've only a daughter to pencil her brow?

Lady Zhen: Don't worry, my lord, now
A worthy son-in-law is as good as a son.

Du (With a smile): Do you think there could be a worthy one?

Lady Zhen: He'll glorify the house, as ancients say,
Do not complain! We're only in the middle of our way.

Together: Let's raise our cup.
After a daughter will a son come up.

Du: Take the tray away, my dear. (Exit the Belle with the tray of wine cups.) Now Fragrant Spring, what is your young mistress doing all day long in her bower?

Fragrant: She passes her hours by embroidering flowers.

Du: So many flowers?

Fragrant: Besides the flowers, she'll sleep away her hours.

Du: How many hours?

Fragrant: As many as flowers.

Du: Ah! Madame, you have told me what our daughter is doing in floral shade. How could she sleep away her hours? Is that the way you told her to do? Call her back at once!

(Re-enter the Belle.)

Belle: What are you calling me back for, dad?

Du: Fragrant has told me how you have passed your days. How could you have slept away your hours without reading books on your shelves? Don't you know a married daughter would honor her family to know reading matters and good manners? How could your mother forget to tell you that?

(Singing to the tune of ***Jade-adorned Belt***):

Although a frugal life we lead,
I've never forgot to read.
A daughter may live as a guest,
A wife at home should do her best.
Your dad may not be strict with you,
But your mom should tell you what to do.

Lady Zhen (Singing to the previous tune):

Seeing my lass as good as lad,
Though busy, I feel glad
Like a pearl you are our treasure.
Whoever sees you will not feel pleasure?
O daughter dear,
Seeing the front, you should know the rear.
You'd try to understand and feel
What your father has to reveal.

Belle (Singing to the previous tune):

Indulgent parents dear,
I'm not so dull as I appear.
I have just drawn a picture of the swing,
And embroidered love-birds on the wing.
From now on I will spend more time
To read more books in prose or rhyme.

Lady Zhen: That is good, but it would be better to find a governess.

Du: (Singing to the previous tune):

It is not easy for our family to find
A qualified scholar of the best kind.

Lady Zhen: Our daughter need not read all the books of the sage
But learn good manners fit for her age.

Together: Let her be worthy of her family,
And know to spin and speak fluently.

Du: It is not difficult to find a teacher;
But he should be well treated as a preacher.
(Singing the Epilogue)
Our daughter need not too much care,
But for the teacher's meal you'd well prepare.

To serve the state as I intend,
It's all on books that I depend.

Epilogue of the Scene

To a teacher we should be kind.
Like vernal wind he'd wake the mind.
Though in old age I have no son,
We'll have a daughter second to none.

Scene 4 A Scholar's Complaint

(Enter Chen Zuiliang.)

Chen (Singing to the tune of ***Double Toast***):

Reading by windowside and in candlelight,
How could a bookworm turn from dull to bright?
I failed in exams again and again;
I am afraid I've wasted time in vain.
What is the use of reading books?
Asthma retains me in my nooks.
Ill, I can't drink much wine;
Poor, I've not much to dine.
How could a man ascend the sky?
A white-haired man can only sigh.

I am Chen Zuiliang, scholar of Nan'an Prefecture. My grandfather practised medicine, and I studied Confucian classics early in my life. At twelve I entered the county school and then I received an additional stipend. Having taken part in fifteen exams during forty-five years, I turned out to be the last in the last exam and was turned out of the school. What is worse, I have been out of job for two years, and have to earn a meagre living, so I am nicknamed Chen the Meagre or Mealless. As I know something in medicine, divination and geomancy, I am called Chen Good-for-Nothing. As I shall be sixty by next year, I don't think I have any more great expectations than running the drugstore left by my grandfather. When a teacher becomes a beseecher, you know what it means. It was said yesterday that Prefect Du was looking for a tutor for his daughter, and many would vie for this job. Why are here so many applicants? First, a tutor of the prefect's daughter may show off his qualification; secondly, he may have some connections with the prefect; thirdly, he may win support from the authority; fourthly, he may collaborate with the steward and servants in intrigues; fifthly, he may brag so as to be promoted; sixthly, he may bully inferior officials, and lastly he may cheat his own family. For these seven things, what won't they do to win the job? But they do not know it is not easy to work in the prefect's house, and still more difficult to teach a girl student. You can neither be too lenient nor too severe with her. If anything goes wrong with her manners, you can neither cry it out nor laugh it off. Only an old scholar like me knows how to solve the dilemma.

Book in hand, I can teach with closed eyes;
Without medicine, I can make the sick rise.
(Enter a courier.)

Courier: How can a scholar not be poor?
But old couriers know more and more.
(Seeing Chen) Congratulations, Master.

Chen: What for?

Courier: Prefect Du is looking for a tutor for his daughter. Our director has recommended a dozen of scholars, but none of them meet the requirements of the Prefect who would have an experienced teacher. Then I mentioned you to our director, and here is the invitation from the Prefect.

Chen: Trouble begins when each has much to teach.

Courier: Trouble ends when each has much food to eat.

Chen: Then let us go at once.

(Singing to the tune of ***Fairy in a Cave*** while they walk)

My hood should be sewn when it is torn,

And my shoes mended when outworn.

Courier: You don't work in the court;

Your long gown becomes short.

Together: Don't rinse your mouth with ink!

Or the rice you eat would stink,

And your toothpick would smell

Alas! not so well.

Courtier: I've found a job for you.

Won't you pay me what's due?

Chen: You ask for a small fee.

Would the Prefect retain me?

Courier: On festive days

You will be invited always.

Bring something out, and don't be late!

Here we are at the Prefect's gate.

Epilogue of the Scene

Courier: Fickle are glory and delight.

Chen: Who cares for the hair silver-white?

Courier: When the Prefect enjoys his leisure,

Together: Who won't curry favor with pleasure?

Scene 5 The Tutor Selected

(Enter Du Bao with attendants.)

Du (Singing to the tune of ***Silk-washing Stream***):

Warm mountain hue,
Lawsuits are few.
Birds fly away at dawn,
And come back at nightfall.
Curtains undrawn,
Petals fall in the hall.
The governor is beyond me;
I'll do as the sage under a pear tree.
So much good for the living and the dead I've done,
Still I have not a jade-like son.

Since I came to Nan'an as prefect, only my wife and my daughter have kept me company. It is now necessary for me to select a tutor for my daughter's education. Yesterday, the director of the prefectural school recommended a sixty-year-old scholar Chen Zuiliang to teach my daughter on the one hand, and to keep me company on the other. Since we are not busy today, I have ordered a feast to entertain the tutor. Now attendant!

Attendant: Yes, my lord.

(Enter Chen Zuiliang wearing a scholar's hood and a blue gown.)

Chen (Singing to the previous tune):

In spirits high

And shabby gown,
Though old am I,
I'll play it down.

Attendant (Announcing): **Here comes Master Chen.**

Du: Invite him to come in.

Attendant: Come in please, Master Chen.

Chen (Kneeling, rising to his feet, bowing and kneeling again.):

I pay my respect to my lord.

(Kowtowing) You have opened the school.

Du: Today let's drink our full.

Chen: Here are cups for the toast.

Du: The guest's honored the host.

Let the attendants withdraw and a houseboy come to the service.

(Exeunt attendants. Enter a houseboy.)

(To Chen) **I have heard of you as a scholar. May I inquire about your age and family?**

Chen (Singing to the tune of ***Southern Branch***):

I am over sixty years old,
And of seventy on the threshold.
Wearing the scholar's hood,
White-haired, I'll teach for food.

Du: What are you doing recently?

Chen: Most scholars know the art to cure,
A gourd at door is a sign sure.

Du: So your family knows the medical art?

What else?

Chen: I can play various parts
And know something about all arts.

Du: So much the better.

(Singing to the previous tune):

Your fame is high, but our acquaintance late,

You're a famed scholar in a famed state.

Chen: I am unworthy of my fame.

Du: My daughter knows to read and write,

She will be instructed with delight.

Chen: It is a teacher's duty, but I am afraid I could not be her worthy tutor.

Du: You can make the pearl

In my palm a learned girl.

It is lucky for her to pay

Her respect to you today.

Attendant, strike the clappers to call your young mistress in.

(Enter Du the Belle with her maid Fragrant Spring)

Belle (Singing to the previous tune):

With eyebrows pencilled green,

My pendants ring when I come in

From behind the embroidered screen.

With lotus steps I come into the hall

To answer my father's call.

Fragrant: What shall we do now the tutor has come?

Belle: I must go to salute him, Fragrant Spring.

Fair maidens model themselves on ladies of old.

Knowing some books, you are a maid of good household.

Attendant (Announcing): Here comes our young mistress.

(Belle greets her father.)

Du: Come over here, my dear.

Unpolished jade cannot be bright;

Unlearned maid knows not what is right.

Come and pay respect to your tutor at this lucky hour.

(Drum beats and trumpets are heard.)

Belle: Like willow down, how dare I to compare

With your students as peach blossoms as fair?

Chen: You are as worthy as a pearl.

I'm honored to teach a jade-like girl.

Du: Fragrant Spring, come and kowtow to Master Chen. Fragrant Spring will accompany her young mistress in her studies. (Fragrant Spring kowtows.)

Chen: May I ask what books our young mistress has read?

Du: She has learned *the Four Books* by heart. It would be better to read the *Five Classics* now. But the *Book of Change* on the sunny and the shady side would be too philosophical and the *Book of History* too political for young maidens. *Spring and Autumn Annals* and *the Book of Rites* seem fragmentary. The *Book of Poetry* which begins with *Cooing and Wooing* is easy to read and its four-character lines easy to learn by heart. Besides, it is our traditional reading, so let her study *Poetry*. We still have many other books, but they are not fit for maidens.

(Singing to the previous tune):

Nearly fifty years old, I'm fond of books,

Having over thirty thousand in my nooks.

It is a pity that I have no son,

To carry on our tradition there is none.

Dear Master, my daughter has all the books she needs. If she has done anything wrong, please punish her maid.

Fragrant: Alas!

Du: When my daughter comes of age,

She should be worthy of family heritage.

You know of course what should be done

Against the naughty one.

Fragrant Spring, accompany your young mistress back. I shall have a drink with our tutor.

Belle: Our tutor may drink wine

To make his student scholar fine. (Exeunt.)

Du: Let us go to the back garden and have a drink.

Epilogue of the Scene

Du: In private school the tutor teaches at leisure.

Chen: For a hundred years scholars eat but rice with pleasure.

Du: I'll make a son of my daughter in her bower.

Together: A teacher is sought for from flower to flower.

ACT II

Scene 1 A Gloomy Outlook

(Enter Han Zicai, descendant of Han Yu.)

Han (singing to the tune of ***Foreign Divination***):

Under the Dynasty of Tang
My ancestor Han Yu was banished to Chaoyang.
Now on Southern Gazebo I hear the sea roar.
Could I as the roc soar?
"The Gazebo overlooks the hay;
Waves from the Sea Gate roll away.
Where are songs and dance of long ago?
I see but partridges flying to and fro."

I am Han Zicai, descendant of the great Tang scholar Han Yu, who was banished to the seaside for his proposal against Buddhist superstition. On his way he was stopped by snow at the Blue Pass, and he thought it was a bad omen. Just then his nephew Han Xiangzi, who became one of the eight immortals, came in rags. At this sight he became all the more unhappy and wrote a poem which ends by two lines for his nephew:

You have come from afar and I know what you mean:
Not to leave my bones there where flow miasmal waves green.

Xiangzi put this poem into his sleeve with a long laughter and disappeared in the blue sky. Then Han Yu died of miasma at Chaozhou without a relative by his bedside. When Xiangzi riding a cloud passed overhead, he recalled this poem, descended to collect his remains and carried them to his hometown, where he happened to meet with his former wife, who aroused his human desire and a son was born to carry on the family line, of which I am a direct descendant. As a result of the turmoil at the time, I moved to the southern town of Guangzhou. Out of respect for my great ancestor, the government conferred on me the title of heir scholar at the Temple of Han Yu. Now I dwell near the Southern Gazebo.

Though beggarly I may appear,
My ancestor was noble peer.

Ah! a friend of mine is coming up, Who can it be?

(Enter Liu Dreamer of Mume Flower.)

Liu (Singing to the previous tune):

Versed in classics I seem,
Tired after a day dream.
To view the clouds I mount the height,
And find the sea like mirror bright.

(They greet each other.)

Han: It is you, my dear Lover of Spring. What wind has brought you to me?

Liu: My roaming propensity leads me here.

Han: At this gazebo you can gaze at the beau.

Liu: If not in spirits high, how can I climb so high?

Han: Then am I ever in high spirits?

Liu: No so high as...

Han: As who?

Liu: As Zhao Tuo gazer of the beau.

(Singing to the tune of ***Cold Window Locked***):

The Emperor of Dragon died,

Deer chasers ran on Central Plain so wide.
But Zhao Tuo who relied
On the ramparts he occupied,
Declared himself sole hero in command
Of the precipitous land,
And built palaces side by side.
But do we scholars have a patch of land
For our free hand?
We've read our fill.
But we possess nor hill nor rill.

Together: Could we rely
On earth or sky?
It is in vain
Of the past or the present to complain.
What can we see
But old gazebo and withered tree?

Han: Judging by what you say, you seem depressed. Do not forget what my ancestor said:
"Do not say others are not right
If you cannot write.
It is not that others are unjust,
But that you've not done what you must."
Perhaps we still have something to learn.

Liu: Do not mention it. You remember my ancestor Liu Zongyuan and yours Han Yu were both learned scholars. Even they could not escape from misfortune. Your ancestor was banished to Chaozhou for his proposal against Buddhist superstition, while mine to Liuzhou for his chess-playing with the prime minister displeased the emperor. It was said that on their way to the miasmal regions, they met in a tavern and had a lampside talk. Your great grandfather said that both yours and mine were comparable in their works as well as in their misfortune. Yours wrote *The Story of a Bricklayer* while mine that of *A Carpenter*, yours the history of a minister while mine that of a gardener; yours *An Elegy to the Crocodile* and mine *Memoir of a Snake-Catcher*. What is more, when your ancestor tried to curry the imperial favor by glorifying the victory on the region south of River Huai, mine dedicated a hymn to the triumph. They shared weal and woe alike, vied from one work to another, and at last were both banished to the miasmal regions at the same time. Was it not predestined? Let us forget the past fortune and misfortune, and talk about the present. My ancestor has left *A Prayer for Talent* but no talent whatever appears in the twenty-eight generations his descendents; nor *Farewell to Poverty* left by yours has rid over twenty generations of your family of poverty. So how can we not be resigned to our destiny?

Han: You are right, dear Lover of Spring.

(Singing to the previous tune):

You have bought books with so much gold.

Don't you know they're worthless when sold?

Nevertheless, when a learned scholar Lu Jia of Han Dynasty came here on imperial errand to confer on Zhao Tuo the title of prince, how richly he was recompensed!

When he returned to the capital,

His carts were loaded with gold, one and all.

At first, the first emperor of Han Dynasty disliked scholars and would piss on the hood of a scholar coming for an audience. When Lu Jia came in a square hood and a dark gown, the emperor thought to himself. Here comes another piss-pot. So he said in a haughty air: "I have conquered the world on horseback". What is the use of your books and verses for me? But Lu Jia was witty enough to retort: "Your Majesty may conquer the world on horseback, but can you rule over it still on horseback?" On hearing this question, the emperor was at a loss, so he said with a broad smile: "Do you think then your books could rule over it? Read me a passage you think fit to the purpose." Then Lu Jia took out without haste a scroll from his sleeve and read aloud the first chapter of his *New Proposals* composed by windowside or in lamplight. The emperor, delighted, broke into broad smiles again and asked him to read one chapter after another, and applauded all the thirteen chapters and ennobled him with the title of Interior Marquis. This glorification won the acclamation and applause of all ministers and generals, who shouted: "Long live the emperor!"

Liu (Sighing): But no one would applaud my works.

Together:

Could we rely
On earth or sky?
It is in vain
Of the past or the present to complain.
What can we see
But old gazebo and withered tree.

Han: Then may I ask you, dear Lover of Spring, how are you earning a living now?

Liu: I am boarding with my gardener.

Han: In my opinion, you had better find a patron to help you.

Liu: Who would be interested in a man of letters now?

Han: Don't you know an imperial envoy for treasure appraisal appraise men of letters as well as treasure? Before his term of office ends in autumn, he will come as usual to assess treasure in the Temple of Fragrant Bay Why don't we go there and pay him a visit?

Liu: All right. Let us have a try.

Epilogue of the Scene

How can a lonely scholar be free from woe?
How could he up to Heaven go?
A prince would be proud of what he has done,
The successful is not the learned one.

Scene 2 Private Lesson

(Enter Chen Zuiliang.)

Chen (Singing): I rewrite last spring's verse which pleases me,

After lunch, I think of drinking afternoon tea.

An ant creeps on my table around the inkwell;

A bee comes for a vase of flowers in my cell.

Private tutor to the young mistress in the prefectural residence, I teach her Book of Poetry, and I am well entertained by the lady of the prefecture. Now breakfast is over, I'll review the notes to the lesson. (Reading the first verse of the *Book of Poetry*):

By riverside are cooing

A pair of turtledoves.

A good young man is wooing

A fair maiden he loves.

Cooing is the soft sound made by the gentle birds and wooing is winning over by saying or doing nice things. (Looking up) **It is late now. Why the young mistress has not yet shown up? She must have been spoiled. Let me strike the clappers.** (Striking the clappers thrice)

Fragrant Spring, ask your young mistress to come for lessons.

(Enter Du the Belle followed by her maid Fragrant Spring with books in hand.)

Belle (Singing to the tune of ***Around the Pool***):

Having dressed up, I come down to the classroom bright;

I'm glad to see the clean desk in window light.

Fragrant: Books of such kind
Would jail the mind.
They are not fit for me,
But for a parrot to call for tea.
(They salute Master Chen.)

Belle: My best wishes and a hundred blessings to you!

Fragrant: My best wishes for you not to chide me!

Chen: A girl student should get up at cock's crow, wash her face, rinse her mouth, brush her teeth, comb her hair and pay respect to her parents. When the sun is up, she shall attend to her work. Now your work is to study, so you must get up early.

Belle: I will not be late any more.

Fragrant: And I will not go to bed tonight but wait at midnight for you to teach us.

Chen: Have you gone over the verse I taught you yesterday?

Belle: Yes, I have. Will you please explain it today?

Chen: Read the text first.

Belle: By riverside are cooing
A pair of turtledoves.
A good young man is wooing
A fair maiden he loves.

Chen: Now listen please. Turtledove is a bird which represents love and cooing its love call.

Fragrant: How will it call?

(Chen imitates the cooing and Fragrant echoes with a funny sound.)

Chen: The turtledove is a gentle bird living by the riverside.

Fragrant: Oh, I understand. I remember it happened yesterday or the day before, this year or last year, that a turtledove kept in the cage was set free by our young mistress and it flew to the river and sighed.

Chen: Nonsense! A pair of turtledoves is evocative. It will make us think of a pair of lovers.

Fragrant: A pair of what?

Chen: The lovers may be a young man and a fair maiden, or a prince and a princess.

Fragrant: Why are they in love?

Chen: Shut up! You ask too much.

Belle: Dear master, I can read the notes and try to understand the verse. Will you please just give me a general idea of the *Book of Poetry*?

Chen (Singing to the tune of ***Changing Roles***):

Of the Six Classics the Book of Poetry is true
To life, It shows what a noble lady should do.
The story of the Lord of Corn
Tells her not to forget by whom she's born.
She should be pious to her mother,
And not be jealous of another,
Be virtuous as a queen Whenever she is seen.
At cock's crow she should rise,
and grieve when swallow away flies.
She may shed tears by riverside
To see her sister cross the river wide.
She would wash powder off her face
And live with grace.
She'd be a faithful wife

And lead a virtuous life.

Belle: Are there so many things to learn?

Chen: The three hundred poems in the *Book of Poetry*, in a word, teach you to do no wrong. So much for the explanation of the text. Now, Fragrant, go and fetch the stationary set for your young mistress to practise hand-writing.

(Exit and re-enter Fragrant Spring with a new stationary set.)

Fragrant: Here they are: paper, ink, brush and inkwell.

Chen: What kind of ink is this?

Belle: Fragrant has mistaken for ink the dye for pencilling the eyebrow.

Chen: What kind of pen is this?

Belle: This is the pencil for painting the eyebrow.

Chen: I have never seen such ink and such pen. Take them away! Take them away! What kind of paper is this?

Belle: This is the paper for billet doux.

Chen: Take it away! Take it away! Bring the writing paper only. What kind of ink slab is this? Is there one hole or two?

Belle: This is the ink stab for lovebirds.

Chen: Why are there so many holes?

Belle: Water may flow through the holes as tears from the eyes.

Chen: Why should tears be shed? Go and change the whole set.

Fragrant (Aside): What an old boor! What can I do but go and change it?

(Exit and re-enter with a new set.) Will this do?

Chen (Examining it): All right.

Belle: I know how to copy the characters. Will you please help Fragrant do hers?

Chen: I will watch how you copy the characters.

(Surprised at her hand-writing.)

I have never seen such good hand-writing. Who is the master you are imitating?

Belle: I imitate the handwriting of Lady Wei.

Fragrant: May I imitate your handwriting?

Belle: It is still too early for you to imitate mine.

Fragrant: May I beg leave to the toilet? (Exit.)

Belle (To Master Chen): May I ask about the age of your respectable wife?

Chen: She is sixty years old.

Belle: I would like to embroider a pair of shoes for her on her sixtieth birthday. May I know the size of her shoes?

Chen: Thank you. Please do according as Mencius said, "You may make shoes without knowing the feet."

Belle: Why is Fragrant Spring not yet back?

Chen: Shall I call her back?

(Calling her thrice. Re-enter Fragrant Spring.)

Fragrant: Damned! Here I am.

Belle (Angry): Where have you been, naughty maid?

Fragrant: Out of the toilet, I have found a large garden with beautiful flowers and grass.

Chen: Ah! You were playing truant in the garden. See how I would punish you!

Fragrant: What should I be punished for?

(Sing to the previous tune):

A maid need not be a student bright.

It is enough for me to learn to read and write. (Standing up.)

Chen: In olden days a student might

read in the moonlight.

Or even open their eyes
To read by the gleaming fireflies.

Fragrant: The moon not bright
Would hurt the sight.
And a firefly
Kept in bag would die.

Chen: But a student would tie
His hair and stab his thigh.

Fragrant: What is the use to hurt his thigh and hair?
He would feel pain and leave scars there. (A flower seller's cry heard.)
Have you heard the seller of flowers?
He is disturbing us in the bowers.

Chen: **Again you are diverting your young mistress' mind. See how I'll punish you.**

(Raising the cane in his hand.)

Fragrant (Dodging): **Beat here!**
In a garden of plum and peach,
If you beat a maid, how can you teach?
(Snatching the cane and throwing it on the ground.)

Belle: **You naughty maid! How dare you offend the tutor!**
Down on your knees!
(Fragrant kneels.)
(To Master Chen) **Would you please excuse her for the first time, and allow me to punish her for you?** (Singing to the previous tune):
Don't touch the garden flowers with your hand,
Nor tread on pathways of the garden land!

Fragrant: **Wait and see if I will.**

Belle: **How dare you retort!**

The incense stick may scorch the mouth of a maid;
The needle may prick your eyes, are you not afraid?

Fragrant: Do you need a blind maid?

Belle: I'll make you by the table stand,
And grind the ink with your hand.
You should recite the verse we read,
And what Confucius said,
And no mistake should be made.

Fragrant: What if I make a mistake?

Belle (Seizing Fragrant by the hair.)
Don't you know how much of your hair will be torn?
How many strokes of the whip on your back will be borne?
You know my mother punishment severe.

Fragrant: I dare not play truant again.

Belle: Now you know it.

Chen: Well, forgive her for the first time. Stand up.
(Fragrant rose to her feet)
(Singing the ***Epilogue***):
Girl students need not strive to be known,
Unlike boy students striving for renown.
You may go back when you have done your class work. I am going to have a talk with your father.

Together: Do not waste time by window light
And with the new gauze screen in sight. (Exit Chen.)

Fragrant (Pointing at Chen's back and railing): An old boor ignorant of young maidens, so tasteless and humorless!

Belle (Pulling her by the sleeve): Naughty maid, don't you know that your teacher for a day would be your father as long as you live?

Why could he not chide and beat you? By the way, where is the garden you have just talked about?

(Fragrant would not answer and Belle put on a smile and asks again.)

Fragrant (Pointing): Just over there.

Belle: Any sight to see?

Fragrant: If you want to see sights, there are a lot in the garden. You will find five or six pavilions and bowers, one or two garden swings, a meandering stream winding along rocky hills, beautiful flowers and grass you have never seen before. What sights for the eyes!

Belle: How could there be such sights without our knowledge? But now, let us go back to our bower.

Epilogue of the Scene

Belle: I can write verse as Poetess of days gone by.

Fragrant: But we can't go to the garden like a butterfly.

Belle: Don't ask how much the boundless spring would bring us woe!

Together: How could we in the shady green forever go?

Scene 3 The Garden

(Enter Fragrant Spring.)

Fragrant (Singing to the tune of ***Breeze-rippled River***):

I'm Fragrant Spring,
More than a maid
Taking care of everything.
Attention paid
To my young mistress,
Her make-up and her dress,
I often by her dressing table stand,
Arranging flowers with my hand.
Together we do embroidery in the hall,
And burn incense at nightfall.
But the old dame
Says always I'm to blame.
"A maiden in her teens is blossoming;
Love will awake in her heart when comes spring.
She'll wait till comes a gallant butterfly,
Then they will go step by step, eye to eye."

I keep company with my young mistress day and night. Though she is a beauty of the country, she is decent and prudent to keep her family honor. Her young face looks tender and shy, yet she appears more dignified than her age. When the tutor engaged by our lord taught her the *Book of Poetry*, she sighed at the verse *A good young man is wooing a fair maiden he loves.* Closing the book, she said, here we can see the heart of a sage and the feeling shared alike by the ancients and the modern. Seeing her a bit tired, I suggested to take it easy and have fun. Hesitating for a moment, she rose and asked me how to have fun and while away the time. I said I knew of no other way than strolling in the back garden. She was afraid our lord would not allow her. Then I reminded her that our lord has been visiting the countryside for a few days. Bowing her head, she thought it over and consulted the calendar, saying that the next day will not do, nor will the day after, but the third day is good, for a minor god will go on a trip on that day So she ordered me to tell the gardener to clean the garden. I answered yes at once, though at heart I feared it might be known to our old lady. But what could be done? I can only leave it to the gardener. Ah! Here comes Master Chen along the corridor.

Oh, how enjoyable springtime should be!
But old bookworms having eyes do not see.

(Enter Master Chen.)

Chen (Singing to the previous tune):

A scholar in old age
Teaches what says the sage.
The curtain waves in vernal breeze,
On the corridor stands a maiden at ease.
She seems to seek a word to speak.
I'll go and see who it can be.
Oh, it is Fragrant Spring
For what is she there lingering?

Where is our lord, where is our lady dear?

Why has not our young mistress come to study here?

Fragrant: Oh, it is you, Master Chen. My young mistress has no time to study these days.

Chen: How could it be so?

Fragrant: Please listen to me!

(Singing to the previous tune):

What season is it now?

How could a learned scholar know not how

To pass spring days?

Chen: In which way?

Fragrant: Master Chen, you do not know that our lord is dissatisfied with you.

Chen: Why?

Fragrant: Please lend me your ear! Our lord said that your lecture was so moving that the verse you explained has moved the heart of our young mistress.

Chen: I have just begun with the *cooing turtledoves.*

Fragrant: That is the point. My young mistress said that even a turtledove would woo by the riverside. How could a man not woo as the bird? On the one hand, a student should bury his head in books; on the other hand, he should raise it to enjoy natural scenery. Now she has told me to get ready for a visit to the back garden in a day or two.

Chen: Why should she visit the back garden?

Fragrant: She is grieved at the departure of spring, and would assuage her grief by a visit.

Chen: So much the more unreasonable.

(Singing to the previous tune):

A woman should stay in her place;
Going out she should veil her face.
It is against the rite
To be exposed to public sight.

Fragrant Spring, I am sixty now, but I have never been grieved for the departing spring, nor delighted at a visit to the garden.

Fragrant: Why not?

Chen: Don't you know what the sage says? In a word, man should set his heart at ease.

If we feel in a garden not overjoyed.
How can we be at its departure annoyed?

Since your young mistress will not come to class, I shall take my leave for a few days.

Fragrant spring, you should come now and then to the classroom,
To clean the broidered window with a broom,
Come here and have a look
If swallows soil with clod the book,

I am leaving now.

"Fair maidens play games of grass in their bowers;
Old scholars won't enjoy the garden flowers." (Exit.)

Fragrant: Thank Heaven, Master Chen is gone. Where is the young gardener? (Calling)

Gardener! (Enter a young gardener a little drunk.)

Gardener (Singing to the tune of ***All Good***):

Since my young days I take care of flowers sweet,
And sell some in stealth on the street.
But officers high or low, two or three,

Would catch hold of me.

When drunken with strong liquor, I'm carefree.

(Greeting Fragrant Spring) Here you are, dear Fragrant.

Fragrant: Do you want to be beaten for slipping out to the street for a drink? Why have you brought no vegetables in for days?

Gardener: There is the green grocer.

Fragrant: Then why have you carried no water to the house either?

Gardener: There is the water carrier.

Fragrant: Then is it your duty to send in flowers?

Gardener: I send in flowers every morning, one bunch for our old lady, and another for our young mistress.

Fragrant: Where have you sent the third bunch?

Gardener: Oh! I am to blame.

Fragrant: What is your name?

Gardener: I am just called Gardener.

Fragrant: If you can make up a song to sing of the gardener, I will spare you the whip.

Gardener: All right, see if I can please you.

(Singing to the tune of ***Pear Flowers***):

I say a gardener is not a car tender,

You say he is not a bar tender.

Both of us say he is not a carpenter

But a guard tender.

Fragrant: I will make up another song.

(Singing to the previous tune):

A gardener will piss on a car tender.

And a car tender on a bar tender.

What if I sing your song to our lord on his return? (Seizing him by the hair) I am afraid you will get beaten and become a guard tender.

Gardener: Excuse me. May I ask what has brought you to the garden?

Fragrant: Our young mistress will pay a visit to the garden the day after tomorrow. Clean the garden paths and get ready for her visit.

Gardener: Yes, I will.

Epilogue of the Scene

How fragrant Eastern flowers are!
On out town shine the Woman Star.
If young men love the powdered face,
They would prattle with a bad grace.

Scene 4 An Enchanting Dream

(Enter Du the Belle with her maid Fragrant Spring.)

Belle (Singing to the tune of ***Around the Pool***):

Awakened by the orioles' song from a dream quiet,
I find spring everywhere run riot.
I stand in the secluded courtyard small
In front of the painted hall.

Fragrant: The incense burned in shreds,
Scattered here and there lie silk threads.
Will spring appear
As mindful as last year?

Belle (Singing to the tune of ***Crows Crying at Night***):

I'm lost in gazing on Mume Pass at dawn,
Still in night gown.

Fragrant: With chignon in spring style,
You lean on the balustrade wearing a smile.

Belle: Ennui won't break.
Put in order, it will make
A mess for no one's sake.

Fragrant: I have told orioles and swallows to weave a spring scene for your eyes.

Belle: Fragrant Spring, have you told the gardener to clean the garden?

Fragrant: Yes, I have.

Belle: Go and fetch my mirror and robe.

(Exit and Re-enter Fragrant Spring with mirror and robe.)

Fragrant: Gazing on the mirror after you comb your hair,
And then perfume the robe you are to wear.
Here are the mirror and your robe.

Belle (Singing to the tune of ***Charming Step by Step***):
The day is fine, willow threads sway and swing,
The leisurely courtyard pervaded with spring.
I pause wordless
To adjust my headdress.
The mirror steals half a glance at my face,
My cloudlike curls slip out of place.
(Walking) Pacing in the bower on my strength,
Could I display my beauty in full length?

Fragrant: You look beautiful in today's dress.

Belle (Singing to the tune of ***Drunkard's Return***):
You see my skirt emerald green and ruby red,
My hairpin sparkling with jewels on my head?
The love of beauty is inborn with me,
Why is beauty inborn for no man to see?
On seeing me, fish would feel shy,
And wild geese come down from the sky,
The moon would close her eye,
Flowers with me can't vie.

Fragrant: It is already time for the morning tea now, let us go.
(Walking.) **You see**
The painted veranda with golden powder bright,
The mossy poolside bowers green our sight.
Treading on grass, you fear your new shoes might he soiled,

To scare birds away from flowers, golden bells have toiled.

Belle: If I did not come to the garden, how could I know spring's splendor?

(Singing to the tune of ***Silk Robe***):

A riot of deep purple and bright red,

What pity on the ruins they overspread!

Why does Heaven give us brilliant day and dazzling sight?

Whose house could boast of a sweeter delight?

What beautiful scenery!

Why have my parents never mentioned it to me?

Together: At dawn on high

Rainbow clouds fly;

At dusk the green

Pavilion is seen.

In misty waves mingle the threads of rain,

The wind swells sails of painted boats in vain.

For those behind the screen

Make light of vernal scene.

Fragrant: All flowers are in bloom, but it is still early for the peony.

Belle (Singing to the tune of ***Good Sister***):

Be not unsatisfied with what you have not seen.

What even if you've seen twelve bowers scene on scene?

Better to leave when you've enjoyed your fill

Than lingering there still.

Fragrant (Singing on arrival):

"I open the doors east and west,

And smooth the bed for you to rest

I put in vase azalea flowers

And burn incense to perfume the bowers."

My young mistress, will you take a rest while I go in to see if our lady needs me? (Exit.)

Belle: After touring the vernal place,

See if my dress becomes my face.

Oh, spring, you come into my heart.

What could I do to see you part?

What annoying weather! Where is Fragrant Spring?

(Looking left and right and sinking in meditation.)

O Heaven! Now I believe spring is stirring the heart. I have read in long or short poems of ancient days that maidens were moved in spring and grieved in autumn. Now I understand the reason why. I'm sixteen years of age, but where is the young man who would win the laureate for me, or fly up to the moon to woo the beauty in the silver palace? Where is the poet to write a love verse on the maple leaf and send it afloat to me? I have read the story of *Red Leaf* and the *Western Bower* in which the talent begins by a tryst and ends in a happy wedding with the beauty.

(Sighing) Born and bred in an official family, I have reached the age of dressing my hair like a bride. But where is the bridegroom? I am wasting the prime of my life and let time slip away day and night like a galloping peony.

(Shedding tears) How can a young maiden in full bloom pass a floating life like a falling leaf?

(Singing to the tune of ***Sheep on the Slope***):

Oh, how can I get rid of the annoyance of spring?

I hear lovesickness in my heart begin to sing.

Is it a beauty horn in noble house

Must only be in love with a fairy spouse?
Is it a happy pair of heart
Must waste their golden hours far, far apart?
Who knows of whom I'm dreaming and why
Should I pretend to be shy?
Where is my dream gone? To which side?
Has it passed away with spring tide?
Do not delay!
To whom my innermost feeling to say?
Annoyed in life, to whom can I reply?
I can only ask the blue sky.
Tired, I'll lean on the table to take a nap.
(Enter Liu the Dreamer.)

Liu: Orioles warble on fine day;
Men break into broad smile when they are gay.
I follow fallen petals on the stream
As lovers met the fairies in their dream.
I follow the beauty I dream of along the way. How is she lost to my sight? (Looking back)
Ah, my beauty, my beauty!
(Surprised, Belle wakes and meets with Liu.)
I have been looking for you everywhere, and at last find you here. (Belle looking sideways keeps silent.)
Here you are. I happened to see a beautiful willow tree in the garden and I broke off one branch for you. Well known for your verse, will you please write a few lines in its praise?

Belle (Pleased but abashed, about to speak but pausing, sunk in meditation, speaking aside.)

I have never seen him before.
How can I know what he is coming for?

Liu (Smiling): **I am so deep in love with you, my dear.**
(Singing to the tune of ***Red Peach in the Mountain***):
Don't you know floral beauty disappears
With running water and fleeting years?
I have been seeking for you from day to day.
How could I know in your bower alone you stay?
May I have a talk with you?

Belle (Smiling without moving. Liu pulls her by the sleeve):
Where to?

Liu: Beyond the flowers,
Beside the lakeside rocks, far from the bowers.

Belle (Asking in a low voice): **What for?**

Liu (in a low voice): I will unfasten your buttons and belt
So that pressure and pleasure may be felt.
I will bring fresh shower
For your thirsting flower.
(Belle blushes and pushes Liu who comes forward to embrace her.)

Together: Oh, we seem to have met
Somewhere we forget
But now face to face we stand,
Wordless though hand in hand.
(Exeunt with Belle in Liu's arms.)
(Enter Fairy of Flowers with hair tied up in a ball and in a red dress a domed with flowers.)

Fairy: To take good care of flowers is my duty.
How can I bear to see pass away the beauty?

The poet grieves when petals fall in shower.
By rainbow cloud he could dream of the flower.

I am the fairy in charge of the flowers in the back garden of the Prefectural Residence at Nan'an, As the prefect's daughter Belle and Liu the Dreamer are predestined to be man and wife, how could she not be lovesick at the sight of spring splendor? How could Liu the Dreamer not come into her dream? It is my duty to make lovers realize their dream. So I come to make them enjoy their fill. I'll make Liu bring fresh shower for Du's thirsty flower.

(Singing to the tune of ***Urging the Old***):

Moonlight evaporates and blends with the sun;
Worm-like, he strives to merge with her into one.
He stirs from above
When stirred by love;
When disarmed,
Her trembling leaflike soul is charmed.
Such is two shadows' love-making.
Two dreamers never waking,
Heart and mind never breaking,
Lust soils the blooming bower.
Let me wake them with falling flower.
(Throwing a fallen flower towards the door of exit.)
The scholar has not loved his fill.
Can I not give him sometime still?
When he wakes from his dreams,
He will see her back with moonbeams.
It's time to leave, I deem. (Exit.)
(Re-enter Du the Belle and Liu the Dreamer hand in hand.)

Dreamer: (Singing to the tune of ***Red Peach in the Mountain***):

By Heaven's order we are wed,
With grass and flowers as our bed.
Are you all right, my love? (Belle lowers her head.)
Your cloudlike hair hangs down;
Your rouge has reddened your gown.
Do not forget, my dear,
When we hugged so near.
I could not tear myself away from you,
Wishing to fuse our flesh and blood anew.
We love until the sun goes down as rouged flower,
And the cloud brings down a fresh shower.

Belle: Are you leaving now, dear Master?

Together: It seems we've met before.
How long it's you whom I adore!
How could together we stay
Without a word to say?

Dreamer: My love, you must be tired. Go and take a rest. Better to have a rest.

(Seeing her fall asleep again.) **My love, I am leaving now.**

(Looking back.) **My love, you must take a good rest, and I will come to see you again.**

I come and bring fresh shower for the fountain;
You go and sleep like cloud over Bewitched Mountain.

(Exit.)

Belle (Startled, waking and murmuring): **Dreamer, Dreamer, am I still dreaming?**

(Dozing off again.) (Enter her mother Zhen.)

Zhen: In golden hall my lord sits down;
By windowside my daughter fair.
On her embroidered gown
There are flowers and birds in pair.
Belle, Belle, why are you dozing here?

Belle (Startled again, waking up and murmuring): Ah! Dreamer, Dreamer!

Zhen: What is the matter with you?

Belle: Oh, it is you, mom!

Zhen: Why are you not occupied with some needlework or some books but doze off here?

Belle: I was enjoying myself in the garden and found springtime annoying. Then I came back to the bower, but found nothing to divert myself, so I fell asleep. Excuse me for not coming out to say my welcome.

Zhen: The garden is not a frequented place. You had better not go there.

Belle: I am sorry for it.

Zhen: Belle, why are you not going to the study?

Belle: The tutor will be absent for a few days, so I may have a few days off.

Zhen (Sighing): My daughter has grown up. She may have her own will. What can I do?
Children when grown up, will be free.
Hard to work for a mother it must be.

Belle (Sighing to see her mother off.): Am I lucky today! Haphazard I were to the garden where flowers in full bloom touched me to the heart, and I returned hopeless and took a nap in my boudoir. Unexpectedly there came a handsome young man of twenty who plucked a twig from the willow tree and asked me to write a verse in its praise. I would have given my assent, but on a second thought, he was not an acquaintance and I did not know his name. How could I venture to speak to him? I was hesitating when he came forward to say something touching, held me tight in his arms and carried me away among the blossoming flowers by the Peony Pavilion and brought fresh shower for my thirsting flower. How enchanting it was when we were merged into one body and soul! When all was over, he saw me back to my boudoir and asked me to take a good rest. I was about to see him off when mother came and woke me up from my sweet dream. I hastened to pay her my respect and listen to her remonstrances, but I made no reply. How could I forget the enchanting dream! I feel at a loss whether to stay or to move. Oh, mom dear, you told me to read books in the study. But what book could divert me from my sweet dream!

(Wiping away her tears.)

(Singing to the tune of ***Cotton Pods***):

The cloud has just brought a fresh shower
To the long-dreaming flower,
When my mother woke
Me up and my dream broke.
I felt my back sticky and wet
With a cold sweat.
My heart seemed altered
And my steps faltered My spirit no longer high,
And my hair went awry.
Though I have done my best,

I could not rise to my feet nor take a rest.
What can I do but go to bed unrest?
(Re-enter Fragrant Spring.)

Fragrant: You may take off your evening gown.
I have already burned the incense down.
My young mistress, may I scent your quilt for you to sleep in?

Belle (Singing the Epilogue):
Tired in spring trip by day,
In unscented bed I would stay.
O Heaven! Would sweet dream not have gone far away!

Epilogue of the Scene

For a free vernal trip I went out of my bower,
What could outvie green willow tree and red mume flower?
Do you know where the lover and the fairy parted?
Awakened by east wind, she'd look back broken-hearted.

ACT III

Scene 1 Mother's Admonition

(Enter Lady Zhen.)

Zhen: "Not so good as yesterday today may appear,
But we grow older this year than last year.
Thinking of my daughter, I sighed.
How could she sit all day by window side?"

Having not been to my daughter's room for a few days, I went to see her at noon, when I found her in low spirit, dozing lonely in her boudoir. She told me she felt tired after a stroll in the garden. Young maidens like her did not know the harm of visiting an unfrequented place in an attractive attire. It must be the maid Fragrant Spring who induced her to go there. Where is Fragrant Spring?

(Enter Fragrant.)

Fragrant: A maid can't take a moment's rest
Without being called east or west.

Madame, you have not gone to bed so late in the night?

Zhen: Where is your young mistress?

Fragrant: After your visit she felt drowsy and murmured herself to sleep. She must be dreaming now.

Zhen: Was it intentional for you to induce her to the garden? What if something harmful should happen?

Fragrant: I would not have dared to do so again.

Zhen: Listen!

(Singing to the tune of ***Conquering the Tartars***):

A maiden should stay in her bower
To embroider grass or flower,
To do more needlework by window side
So as not to waste time and tide.
If she has leisure when lengthens the day,
She may have books to read and music to play.
Why go to the garden? For what need she?

Fragrant: In the garden there are fine sights to see.

Zhen: Fine sights are not so important as long sight. Don't you know? Listen to me!

(Singing to the previous tune):

The garden when deserted is in vain too wide,
With crumbled walls and bowers side by side.
Even the middle-aged would hesitate
Whether they'd go there or just wait.
As for young maidens fair,
It would be lucky to be safe there.

Fragrant: What if unlucky?

Zhen: If there were anything wrong,
The trouble would last long.

Your young mistress did not take her supper today. Breakfast should be served earlier. Tell her what I say to you. (They sing the Epilogue):

Zhen: The evil-doers haunt the woods in wind and shower.

Fragrant: Still there goes the lover to seek for flower.

Zhen: A maiden is not proof against the vice.

Fragrant: She should listen to her mother's advice.

Scene 2 The Dream Retraced

(Enter Fragrant Spring.)

Fragrant (Singing to the tune of ***Night Tour around the Palace***):

Having washed and powdered my cloudlike face,
I put my hairpin aslant in its place.
A chambermaid should early rise,
Though sleepy are her eyes,
Before the wardrobe green.
By the dressing table between
The painted screens.

I am Fragrant Spring, chambermaid attending on my young mistress. Since the appearance of the cat-like master, no mouse is allowed to show off. As luck would have it, my young mistress, moved by the Book of Poetry, chose a day to visit the back garden with me so as to divert herself from ennui. Who knows how she was dozing off when our old lady dropped in and laid blame on her and on me. How dare I venture any protest but plead guilty and promised not to do it again, But Madame would not let it off till I swore...

Voice within: What did you swear, Fragrant?

Fragrant: What could I swear but that I should be punished with a perpetual single life? That saved me from a threatening storm, but how could a phoenix listen to a crow? My young mistress was restless all night long. She got up early and urged me to fetch water for her morning make-up. She murmured to herself until the sun was high and cast the shadows of flowers on the gauzed window.

Voice within: Tell the young mistress that breakfast is served.

Fragrant (Singing): Breakfast is served, it is said,
And tea and soup should be fetched by the maid. (Exit.)

(Enter Belle.)

Belle (Singing to the tune of ***The Moon Is High***):

I knit my eyebrows green
Like the mountain on the screen.
Why should my quilt restrain my tender heart?
My languor comes not from the part
Of the moon's sorrow
To see me in bed till the morrow.
Do I regret the fallen flower,
So early I went out of my bower?
Among the flowers rose a dream,
My chest hove up and down like a stream.
Sleepless in flickering lamplight,
I envied Fragrant's sound sleep all night.

In yesterday's random excursion I did not know who entered into my dream. I gazed at him and could not tear myself away as if we were lifelong companions. Now as I think over it alone, I seem to have fallen into a gloomy whim. What a pity! (Sunk in sullen mood.)

(Enter Fragrant with breakfast in a tea tray.)

Fragrant (Singing): The parrot loves the pearl-like rice;
The tea leaf looks like partridge's feather nice.

Belle: I am in no mood for breakfast.

(Singing to the previous tune):

I have just washed my face and combed my hair,
Leaving the looking glass still there.
I would nor get up nor lie down.
How could I eat food and not frown?

Fragrant: By order of our old lady, the breakfast should be early today.

Belle: My mother only orders the hungry to eat. But don't you know the hungry eat to live while the well-fed live to eat?

Fragrant: I know only to eat three meals a day.

Belle: I find the bowl too heavy to hold.
I seem to have enough, hot or cold.
Take it away and eat it as you are told.

Fragrant: I think the leftover food
As remains of powder as good. (Exit.)

Belle: Now Fragrant has left, but the peony pavilion I dreamed of yesterday has not vanished but revives, and the old dream has brought a new grief. I thought it over and tossed in bed all night without falling asleep. Now Fragrant is not here. Why not take the chance to see the sights in the back garden? It is just like what the poet Li Shangyin says:

Having no wings, I cannot fly to you as I please;
Our hearts at one, your ears can hear my inner call.

Along the way I come to the garden. I find the gate left open and no, gardener in it. What I see is a garden strewn with fallen flowers. (Singing to the tune of ***Eyebrows Idly Pencilled***):

How bewitching is spring this year!
High and low painted walls appear,

Spring stirs the heart far and near. (Stumbling.)
The creeping raspberries won't let me go away;
They seem to lead my heart astray,
See what a winding stream!
(Singing to the previous tune):
Why should lovers retrace the way to their bower?
I see water sprinkle and blossoms fly.
Gods in the sky
Need not pay for the flower.
So they let men shed tears on fallen reds.
And not enjoy the beauty early spring spreads.
(Enter Fragrant.)

Fragrant: **When I come back after breakfast, I cannot find my young mistress. Where can she be? Oh, here you are, my young mistress.** (Singing to the tune of ***Impasse***):
Why should a maiden fair be
Standing by a blooming mume tree?
Just after breakfast, how could you
Visit alone the back garden anew?

Belle: In painted corridor nearby
I saw clod-pecking swallows fly.
My random steps lead me
To visit the garden haphazardly.

Fragrant: Go back at once, I pray,
Or our old lady would say:
"Who told you to go out carefree?
Who told you to go out carefree?"

Belle (Singing to the previous tune): I come here at random;

You seem to say I am wanton.

Fragrant: You are not wanton, but you do want one.

Belle: You take advantage of my good temper. I say I come to the garden, lying down at random, you say I am telling a lie for I want one in the garden.

Fragrant: How dare I tell a lie? I am just telling you what our old lady has told me. She said,

Spring is good for embroidery, and better
To burn incense to scent the letter.

Belle: What else did she say?

Fragrant: The garden lies in waste,
Where fairies and goblins come in throng.
We should go back in haste,
And not tarry too long,

Belle: I see. You go first to assure my mother not to worry about me. I will come after.

Fragrant: Flowers would lean on rocks as ornament.
A bird in cage would voice its discontent. (Exit.)

Belle: Now Fragrant is gone, and I may go to the back garden to retrace my dream.

(Singing to the tune of ***A Wine Song***):

Here are the rocks by the side of the lake,
There is the Peony Pavilion where I did wake.
Here by the balustrade the flowers please,
There thread by thread sway willow trees.
The elm fruit hang like coins in string,
But could they buy back threads of spring?

Here is the place where the seductive Dreamer asked me to

write a verse in praise of the willow twig he plucked off. It seems long, long ago. (Singing to the tune of ***Festive Song***):

Who is the gallant coming from afar at leisure?
Who dared to turn my boudoir into a garden of pleasure?
How could I not feel shy
When his hand stroked my lower eye?
O Heaven high!
I opened my lower lips
For his rewarding dew drips.

(Singing to the tune of ***An official Song***):

How did the young scholar allure!
Were we in the past man and wife?
I am not sure,
Are we acquainted in this life?
I only told him: "I wish to meet with you.
You come into my dream as an acquaintance new,
As a scholar timid and carefree.
How dare you carry me away and sleep with me?"
But how amorous was he!

(Singing to the tune of ***Rank Song***):

He leaned on the rock by lakeside;
I stood like a jade statue vivified.
He carried away his jade mate
Who might in warm sunlight evaporate.
Passing by the balustrade in spring
Around the garden swing.
He pulled down my flowery skirt that I
Might lie on the ground screened by the rock from the sky.

The shortest moment dissolved in the longest time,
Blooming and gloomy, fragrant and sublime!
The dreaming tide is high,
A petal drops down from the sky.
(Singing to the tune of ***Yellow Bean Leaf***):
He made up his mind to hold me tight
And kissed my shoulder with his might.
Slowly I returned his love
Coming from above.
His gallantry made his maid bright
Fall into a sad plight,
So tender and so soft,
With outer garment doffed.
Suddenly fell shower of petals red
Like rainbow cloud in mid-air spread.
Could flower goblins seem
To have come into my dream?
I sought and searched, and found the pavilion in gloom
And flowers in full bloom.
How can it be now so sad and drear
To find no scholar here!
(Singing to the tune of ***Entwined Jade Branches***):
(Shedding tears.)
On such barren wasteland
There's no pavilion nor bower near at hand.
Colorful, it can't be seen by color-blind eye
As the bright sun in the blue sky.
I cannot revive the scene in my dream,

But suddenly how lively it would seem!
I linger for a while,
This Is the place where love mingled with smile.
O but where to see
The dreamer again with me?
(Singing to the tune of the ***Moon over the Crabapple***):
How to win him by a wink?
I seem to see him on the brink.
He came at a slow pace,
And went with lingering grace.
He cannot be far away:
I see the cloud and shower he brought still stay.
I wish he'd reappear, amid willows and flowers
As yesterday before the bowers,
In my heart as before the eye.
The Sunny Terrace high
Would turn into a rendezvous as before,
Where we may renew our love once more.
(Looking around) **Ah! How could a big mume tree suddenly emerge from nowhere, overloaded with mume fruit!**
(Singing to the tune of ***Double Mini-song***):
With gloomy fragrance spread far and wide,
You give a lovely shade for me by your side.
In early spring your fruit reddens the sky
With your leaves in deep dye.
Why should you have a bitter heart?
You seem to have played my part.
How I love your shade by day!

Could I in the dream of your fairyland stay?
I wish you would share your beauty with me.
How fortunate to be buried under your tree!
(Singing to the tune of ***Water in the River***):
I happened to pour out my heart by the mume tree;
I'd like to linger there its flowers to see,
To enjoy life till death without restraint
Or shed tear without complaint.
I'd let my soul dissolve in the mume rain
And wait for him but not in vain.
(Enter Fragrant.)

Fragrant: My mistress visits spring pavilion far away;
Her maid burns incense in her bower by noonday.
Ah! My young mistress is tired in her walk, so she is dozing off under the mume tree.
(To Belle) Why are you leaning against a mume tree and dozing off?

Belle: For a while I turned my eyes
Towards the boundless skies.
I pity myself without knowing why. (Shedding tears.)

Together: We do not know what in our heart appears
Nor what draws forth our tears.

Fragrant: How do you feel, my dear mistress?

Belle (Singing to the previous tune):
I tried to find the trace
Of parting spring and of his face.
We gazed at each other without a word.
But our hearts could be heard.
I should have plucked a willow sprig,

I should have plucked a willow sprig
To ask the sky on high.
I regret now,
I regret now
To have written no verse to the willow's brow.

Fragrant: I cannot guess at your riddle.

Together: We do not know what in the heart appears
Nor what draws forth our tears.

Fragrant: Let us go back then.

Belle (Walking and halting, singing to the previous tune):

Let me go back at a slower pace
And linger still with more grace!
(Birds' song heard from within.)
Listen! why not go back as the birds sing
When late is spring?
Should I come back again,
Should I come back again
To hear the birds' refrain?
Should I come along
To the pavilion for a dream short or long?

Together:

We do not know what in the heart appears,
Nor what draws forth our tears.

Fragrant: Here we are. Shall we go to see our old lady?

Belle: Not now.

(Singing to the tune of ***Endless Love***):
Tired out, I arrive at the balustrade west
When I am told my mother is at rest,

Oh! Belle, you go upstairs to see the bloom.
What could you do but spend a lonely time in gloom!

Epilogue of the Scene

Belle: Where is the Peach Blossom Fountain to find my lover?
Fragrant: It would be a pity to find a forgetful rover.
Belle: From now on in spring dream we'll hear song after song.
Fragrant: But one heart-breaking regret will last life-long.

Scene 3 Departure

(Enter Liu the Dreamer of Mume Flower.)

Liu (Singing to the tune of ***A Skyful of Apricot Flowers***):

Although a scholar of renown,
Hunger is to my belly often known.
Like a lofty mountain fair,
I drink only of fresh air.
I dreamed of splendid palace hall;
Awake, I find a hut with crumbled wall.
A thirsty dragon cannot fly;
Nor can a wingless rabbit climb the sky.
I can draw tigers at my best.
Where can a crow find a branch to rest?

I, Liu the Dreamer, is one of the outstanding scholars in Guangzhou Prefectural School. In scorching summers as well as in freezing winters, I dwell in a shabby house,depending on an old gardener for living. How I feel ashamed to think of it! How I feel ashamed to think of it! My friend Han advised me to go to another county to earn a living. Having only four empty walls, on what can I rely but accept his advice? How could a tree bearing no fruit serve a hungry man? Where is my old gardener?

(Enter Guo, the old gardener.)

Guo (Singing to the tune of ***Double Words***):

The hill in front is low while that in the rear is high:
Hunchback am I.
Shooting an arrow by bending the bow,
Backward I go,
Ten times I have advanced and retired
How much I'm tired!
Sometimes I fall like a ball,
No air in it at all.

I am gardener Guo the Hunchback. My ancestor came to Liuzhou with his master Liu Zongyuan, famous writer of the Tang Dynasty. I follow his descendant, great-grandson of the 29th generation, and we have lived here in time of peace and of war. Now the fruit is sold, I shall inform my young master of that. (Meeting Liu the Dreamer.) My young master, you are diligent as usual.

Liu: My dear Guo, you have come in time, for I have something important to tell you. As I am a scholar of twenty years old, I see no perspective of a bright future. When I think it over, I find there is still a long way to go. How can I spend my life here, living from hand to mouth, busy for food and fuel? I would leave here confiding the garden and trees to you. Now listen to me.

(Singing to the tune of ***Southern Laurel Branch***):

All these years I have relied on you.
How many thanks to you are due!
I have tasted good and bad, sweet and sour,
You have cultivated the fruit and flower.
What do I look like on days fine?
A drunkard indulged in wine.

When could I make your hunchback straight?
Under the tree I can but wait.
Of whom can I complain?
The garden cannot lie waste in vain;
Only you can revive it again.

Guo (Singing to the previous tune):

A hunchback may rely on his hand
To cultivate the garden land.
Though I cannot straighten my legs and waist,
With might and main I won't let it lie waste.

My dear young master, what are you going to do after leaving the orchard?

Liu: I would rather curry favor with a stick than wait for three meals a day.

Guo: How to curry favor with a stick?

Liu: Ask the autumn wind to help me.

Guo: I think it would be better to take the civil service examinations than to go from place to place to curry favor.

Liu: Do you think to ask autumn wind for help is not good?

Don't you know the Martial Emperor of the Han Dynasty curried favor of the autumn wind and wrote his famous *Ode to the Fallen Leaves and Thrilling Cicadas* and became well-known to the posterity?

Guo: My dear young master, do not cite the ancient to prove the modem. Don't you know a favorable wind might bring the poet Wang Bo to Prince Teng's Pavilion and an adverse one might bring thunder to strike a monument asunder?

Liu: I am eager to curry favor from the autumn wind. Do not stand in my way!

Guo: At least you should get your things and luggage ready.

Liu: My shabby dress would win me favor from the autumn wind.

Guo: I wish to see you back in glory.

Epilogue of the Scene

Liu: I'm sad and drear to wander east and west.

Guo: You should see tree on tree at its best.

Liu: Can I justify the trip I'll make as I please?

Guo: The vernal wind will triumph over the autumn breeze.

(Exeunt.)

Scene 4 The Portrait

(Enter Du the Belle.)

Belle (Singing to the tune of ***Break-through***):

Awake from dream of untrodden winding way,
I find my soul in deep boudoir astray.
Like mist-veiled bloom
Or moonlit gloom
My amorous heart looks at break of day.

(Enter Fragrant Spring.)

Fragrant: Afraid to stray like a beauty-seeking butterfly,
I rose to make up and hear swallows cry.
Rosy sleeves call and sing
When comes back spring,

Belle (Singing to the tune of ***Drunk in Peach Blossom Fountain***):

Is it a fancy or a love affair?
For Peony Pavilion do I care.

Fragrant: Heart-broken spring hidden in your eyebrows still,
Who will find it in distant hill?

Belle: How to get rid of grief on grief?
My robe is thin beyond belief.
The blooming branch sheds rosy tears.

Together: It's hard to bring fresh shower
For the fairy's thirsting flower,

Fragrant: My young mistress, since your visit to the garden, you seem not to care for food or sleep. You have grown thin and slender. Does it come from spring grief? Though I know not the reason why, I should suggest not to visit the garden again.

Belle: What do you know about my dream?

A vernal dream is hidden in early spring gloom;
Morning chill lessens one-tenth of flowers in bloom.

(Singing to the tune of ***Prelude to the Brush***)

When cold spring days quietly go,
I care for nothing, being in spirits low,
Dressed up and scented, alone annoyed,
How can I have grief laden weeds destroyed?
For whom should I beguile
True love with forced smile?
My teary would break
Into my dreaming soul for my love's sake.

Fragrant (Singing to the tune of ***A Maid-servant***):

Why will your roaming heart fly so high?
How could your cold tears go dry?
These garden trips have made it clear,
Orioles will warble and swallows twitter here.

Just think it over: what if our old lady should see you thus?
A hundred per cent beauty, if gloomy, would lose ninety percent of it?

Belle: If Fragrant can be believed, I must be ninety per cent languished. I should look into the mirror to see what languor looks like. (Startled when looking into the mirror.) Alas! Where is my beauty of bygone days? If I did not draw a picture of myself, how could the world know once there was such a beauty on earth as the Goddess of Mount Witch? Fragrant, fetch a silk scroll and colors! See how I will draw a portrait of myself.

(Fragrant withdraws and re-enters.)

Fragrant: It would be easier to paint a vernal scene
Than to reveal the lovesickness so lean.
My young mistress, here are the scroll and colors you need.

Belle: Strange it appears
For me to paint my own picture of sixteen years.
(Singing to the tune of ***Universal Joy***):
The beauty of youth looks like flower,
For it will fade from hour to hour,
It is not that youth is unfortunate,
But that such is the rosy face's fate.
There are so many beauties on earth.
But their splendor will soon lose its worth.
If the flames of their love were put down,
They'd be fair as West Lake with the moon as its crown,
And the hills as its gown.
(Singing to the tune of ***Honking Wild Geese***):
(Sighing while looking in the mirror)
The silk so light
Wipes the mirror bright!
Let my brush touch and sweep
Over the scroll with leap on leap!
O my image, let us compare
You with my dimpled cheeks so fair!
My lips cherry-red,
My eyebrows willow-green

And cloudlike hair on my forehead!
The brows so green have never been seen.
My beauty lies in gleaming eyes,
The hill-like brows that rise
And gems and pearls of small size.
Fragrant (Singing to the tune of ***A Cup Dried Up***):
Your smiles that please
And slender waist in the east breeze,
Drowned in spring grief, you seem not at ease.

Belle: See on the scroll the hills and rills,
Three or four gates and doors,
A maiden at leisure
Enjoying pleasure.
With mumes she plays
And beams at what the dreamer says.
She leans on rocks by the lake
Until from dreams she is awake
Or standing under willow trees
With branches swaying in the breeze.
She is so slender
Against palm leaves so tender!
Fragrant, hold up the scroll and see if the portrait looks like me.

Fragrant (Singing to the tune of ***Jade Lotus***):
It's easy to draw pictures of a maiden fair,
But with the person the portrait cannot compare.
It's only like the moon in water of the stream
Or the shadow of a flower in the dream.

Belle (Joyful): **How lovely is the portrait!**

If a picture could be so fair,
The person must be beyond compare.

Fragrant: It is a pity there's no bridegroom by the side
Of the fair future bride,
If you were early wed,
You need not envy bride and groom in nuptial bed.

Belle: Fragrant, to tell the truth, when I visited the garden, I met with a gallant young man.

Fragrant: My dear young mistress, how could it be so convenient?

Belle: It was in a dream.
(Singing to the tune of ***Mountain Peach***):
In the dream a man smiled at me.
I'll tell you how so it could be,
Then I'll describe in detail how charming was he.
But I'm afraid to reveal my innermost love.
His face looks like the moon amid the clouds above.
He must be the winner of the laurel crown.
I remember how he snapped a willow twig down.
Could his name he Liu or Willow
To share with me my pillow?
I've got a poem to reveal my amorous heart.
I will write it on the portrait to show my art.

Fragrant: Nothing could be better.

Belle: "The portrait seems alive when viewed near by;
Viewed from afar, it is a fairy who seems to fly.
If I could be the laurel winner's bride,
It must be by the mume's or by the willow's side."
Since olden days there have been beauties whose admirers

would draw a picture for them or who would draw their own picture for their admirers. But, Fragrant, to whom could I send this portrait of mine?

(Singing to the tune of ***Epilogue Begins***):

Worry appears on my joyful face,
Joyful for my bright dress and grace.
My fairy robe adorned with gems might appear
Too beautiful to outlast the long year,
Hidden in a golden cave none could come near.
Who would for my short-lived beauty shed tear?
How could my admirer call me his dear?
My youth passed away would grieve me the more,
If I left no picture for the future to adore.

Fragrant, call the gardener and tell him what to do.

Fragrant (Calling) Gardener!

(Enter the gardener.)

Gardener: I live all my life long amid flowers
And look unlike a man in bowers.
What are you calling me for?

Belle: Go and have this picture well mounted!

(Singing to the tune of ***Urging the Old***):

The maiden in the picture is fair,
Will you have it mounted with care?
The silk is white
And the space bright.
The margin should be small
So that there's nothing wrong at all.
Can it be proof against the sun and breeze?

Can it hang long with ease?

Gardener: Where shall it hang when it is mounted?

(Singing the ***Epilogue***):

Belle: It cannot be admired if shut up in my bower.

Fragrant: Hang it in temple where the cloud brings showers

For thirsty flower.

Together: But we're afraid

With cloud and rain it will fade.

Epilogue of the Scene

Fragrant: The pearls and jade before the eyes can't please the heart.

Belle: How can I not weep before flowers with them to part?

Fragrant: You paint a charming beauty in a charming scene.

Belle: It might outshine the most beautiful fairy queen.

(Exeunt)

ACT IV

Scene 1 An Inquiry

(Enter Zhen, Lady Du.)

Zhen (Singing to the tune of ***Three Rises***):

How shall I live in the rest of my life?
My daughter may be gone before she's made a wife.
With loneliness I shall then be in strife. (Shedding tears.)
She is the pearl in my heart.
Of my flesh she's a part,
What could I do
If what I fear should come true?
Others may have seven sons to enjoy their fill.
Why should my only daughter fall ill?
(Singing to the tune of ***Pure Serene Music***):
She is so delicate a flower
That Heaven would pity her in her bower.
Why should violent wind and rain
Harass her with might and main?
She should confine herself behind the screen.
Who tells her to be drunk in windy moonlit scene?
My heart is inch by inch half broken;
My tears stream down when I am woken.

I am nearly fifty years old and yet have only one daughter. I do not know why she has been ill for half a year. Judging by her looks and talk, she seems not to have caught a cold. Then what is the matter? The maid must have known it. I will call her for an inquiry. Fragrant!

(Enter Fragrant.)

Fragrant: Here I am. (Singing)

There is no clever boy I have seen with my eyes.
I have to serve my rail mistress who in bed lies.
I hear my old lady call me from the hall.
Is there any wine or rouge left over at all?

I kowtow to Your Ladyship.

Zhen: Your young mistress was in good health half a year before you attended on her. How could she have fallen ill since your service? How could she? How could she? Now tell me about her meals.

Fragrant: (Singing to the tune of ***Listening on Horse***):

She neither eats nor drinks. She won't answer even when asked. She only sheds tears, endures secret pain and laughs it away, then feels at a loss and falls asleep, and wakes up with drowsy eyes or sleep with eyes wide-open.

Zhen: The doctor was sent for three days ago. What did he say?

Fragrant: He used acupuncture, but it could not cure her tender heart. He used magic pills, but how could pills cure her of lovesickness?

Zhen: What is she ill of?

Fragrant: I do not know. (Singing)

She lies in bed when autumn winds sing,
But she suffers from illness of late spring.

Zhen (Sobbing): How could it be so?

(Singing to the previous tune):

How could she grow so slender
And lose the grace the stars would lend her?
It must be you who have induced her to become thus.
Since olden days flowers have played their part;
Orioles and swallows have shown their art,
And the moon and clouds know her heart.
On your knees, you tricky maid! You shall be punished with the rod.

Fragrant (Kneeling): I really do not know the cause.

Zhen: How could you make her jade-like body grow so lean,
And move her mind so keen?

Fragrant: I do not know how she got ill while enjoying flowers and willow trees.

Zhen (Angered): You tricky and talkative maid! See how I shall punish your evil tongue.

Fragrant: Do not hurt your hand, Madame. I will tell you what I know. You remember the day when you came across us coming back from the garden? It is on that day my young mistress told me that a young scholar snapped a twig from a willow tree and asked her to write a verse in its praise. She declined it because he was not an acquaintance.

Zhen: That was all right. What then?

Fragrant: Then the scholar held her in his hands and put her down in his arms and carried her off to the Peony Pavilion.

Zhen: What for?

Fragrant: How could I know it? My young mistress was dreaming.

Zhen (Startled): Was it a dream?

Fragrant: Yes, it was.

Zhen: Then she must have been haunted. We should let it be known to our lord.

Fragrant: Would it please Your Lordship to come out?

(Enter Du.)

Du (Singing): I fear too heavy is my official duty,
Too light the plate of jade to hold a beauty.

Madame, how is our dear daughter? Has she got better now?

Zhen (Sobbing): My lord, will you please lend me your ears?

(Singing to the previous tune):

Talking about how she got ill,
My heart feels painful still.
I see her seldom rise but often asleep.
When she smiles, she seems to weep,
Or like a shapeless shadow trying to peep.

It is because she visited the back garden and dreamed of a young man holding a willow twig and carrying her away. I am afraid her slender waist had offended the willow sprite or the floral fairy. Oh, my lord, would you please pray to the stars that they should shed no light to do her harm!

Du: How could you come to that again! I engaged Master Chen to teach her classics so that she might refrain herself. How could you, as her mother, let her spend her leisure to stroll in the back garden? (Smiling) Now she was warmed by sunshine and then caught cold in the breeze. I do not think she needs any witch to pray to the stars. As the saying goes, if you believe in the witch and not in the doctor, you can cure no illness. I will ask Master Chen to diagnose her pulse.

Zhen: What is the use of diagnoses? If she were betrothed earlier, how could she have been affected by such disease?

Du: It is said in the books that man should get married at thirty and woman at twenty. She has not yet reached womanhood. What could she know about man and wife?

(Singing to the previous tune):

How could our daughter know love at sixteen years old?
She's only affected by alternate heat and cold.
It's all your fault: if you treasure the pearl in hand,
No illness in the heart could she not withstand.

Together (Sobbing): A lonely pair of man and wife
Pray Heaven to bless the treasure of their life,

(Exeunt.)

Epilogue of the Scene

She's ill when the east breeze rises from willow trees;
The whole family grieves with tears shed on the sleeves.
They seek for medicinal herb from helping hand,
Could they meet an immortal in the fairy land?

Scene 2 The Diagnosis

(Enter Belle supported by Fragrant.)

Belle (Singing to the tune of ***Breeze-rippled River***):

Lost in disease,
I languish, ill at ease.
How can I solve the riddle or know the role
Of an enchanted soul?
Awake from dream
As a swallow flits from a stream
Of current and enters the screen,
I feel a grief unseen.
So long has spring departed.
Could I preserve my beauty of years green?
The fallen leaves make me broken-hearted,
(Singing to the tune of ***Pilgrimage***):
With my spirit to make haste,
And my leaf-like slender waist,
Could I from illness be raised?

Fragrant: From your starry eyes
And your rosy face
So much charm would rise
With as much love and grace.

Belle: I love to play with the mume sprig
And he to pluck a willow twig,

I'm drowned in dreams of oldened spring.

Fragrant: The incense burned at noon would bring

A scented pillow in clear breeze.

For whom do you fall in disease?

Why knit your brow,

Grow lean and feel grief now?

Belle: Fragrant, since my spring visit to the back garden, I have been ill up to now, feeling neither itch nor pain as if drunken or lost. How can I know what is the matter?

Fragrant: My dear young mistress, why should you think of your dream?

Belle: How could I not think of it?

(Singing to the tune of ***Golden Lacework***):

For his fond love I've uttered sigh on sigh.

I would not think of it, but how could I?

So I grow thin alone

For fear of being known.

I cough and heave.

Who would believe

Such languor as I confine in my vernal heart?

I regret for my part.

Why should I stay

Spring from going away?

Fragrant: Our old lady has made preparations to drive away the evil spirits from the garden.

Belle: What evil spirits? Are floral fairies evil doers to be driven away?

Fragrant (Singing to the previous tune):

Spring's gone away,

But vernal grief will stay,

Spring is asleep,
The grief in your heart is still deep,
How could short breaths measure long, long days?
Though you knit your brow,
Your disease stays,
My dear young mistress, now
Wake up from your dreams!
You don't even know who is he.
But the longer you're in bed, the weaker you will be.
You wait for floating cloud to bring fresh shower
For your long thirsting flower.
But could your one-sided love
Bring down the cloud from above?
The weather is not bad,
You have no reason to be sad.
(Enter Master Chen.)

Chen (Singing): Sunning my books, I fear but bird;
Pounding the herbs, I need the magic words.
I am Master Chen, ordered by our lord to come to feel the pulse of our young mistress. Coming to the inner hall, I must call for the maid. Is Fragrant there?

Fragrant (Meeting him.): Oh, it is Master Chen. Our young mistress is still asleep in bed.

Chen: Do not disturb her then. I will go in myself. (Greeting her.) My young mistress.

Belle (Startled): May I know who is coming?

Fragrant: It is Master Chen.

Belle (Rising in bed.): Dear Master, Sorry I have been ill so long that I cannot get up to pay you my respects.

Chen: My dear student, don't you know what the ancient told us, "Diligence leads to success in studies and negligence to failure"? As you basked in sunshine and wind in the garden, so you have fallen ill as to neglect your studies. As your master, I feel ill at ease. Now our lord calls me back to make diagnoses, but I did not expect to see you so frail and so weak. Such is the case, I do not know how long it will take for you to resume your studies. I am afraid you could not recover before the Dragon Boat Festival.

Fragrant: Master Chen, you need not worry about your festival gifts.

Chen: I mention the festival without the least idea of the gifts. My dear young mistress, of course you know the four words for diagnoses: "look, hear, ask and feel the pulse." Now may I ask how you fell ill in the beginning?

Fragrant: You need not ask her, for the cause lies in none other than yourself. Do you still remember what you have taught her:

There is a maiden fair
A good young man is wooing?

Chen: Which good young man is wooing her?

Fragrant: How can I know which?

Chen: The illness coming from the *Book of Poetry* can be cured by the verse from the same Book. In the first part of the *Book of Lyrics* you can find the remedy.

Fragrant: Dear Master, do you remember the verse?

Chen: Your young mistress' lovesickness comes from the wooing young man, so it can be cured by the verse from Wind and Rain:

Since I have seen my dear one,
With my illness could not have done?

She would be cured if she could see her dear one.

Belle (Ashamed): Ah!

Fragrant: What else?

Chen: She would be further cured by ten mume fruits for it is said in the *Book of Lyrics*:

The fruits from mume tree fall,
Three-tenths of them away.
The fruits from mume tree fall,
Seven-tenths of them away.

Three and seven makes ten, so ten mume fruits would cure a maiden from lovesickness.

Belle (Sighing): Ah!

Fragrant: Still what else?

Chen: She should be cured under three stars.

Fragrant: Why three?

Chen: No more, for it is said in the *Wedding Song*:

When in the sky three stars appear.

Fragrant: Anything more?

Chen: It is said in the *Woodcutter's Love:*

I would fain feed her horse,
If she should marry me.

So the horse flesh could cure a maiden who would be married.

Fragrant: Master Chen, how could you compare a maiden to a horse?

Chen: A maiden should be fed just as a horse should.

Belle: What a good doctor is Master Chen!

Fragrant: What a bad nurse!

Belle: Dear Master, do not write the prescription now. Please feel my pulse first.

(Chen feels her pulse, but mistakes the part of her wrist.)

Fragrant: Master Chen, would you turn her wrist and feel her pulse?

Chen: According to the *Book of Diagnoses*, if a doctor should feel the pulse of a woman, it is contrary to that of a man, that is, he should put his fingers on the back of her wrist. But it will also do to feel the other side. (Feeling her pulse.) Ah! How could your pulse be weak to such a point!

(Singing to the tune of ***Golden Leaves of the Plane Tree***):

You're such a maiden fair,
But your weak pulse is rare.
In your sweet inner bower,
How could you languish like a fading flower!
(Standing up) Oh, Fragrant,
Your young mistress is grieved at parting spring too sweet
And afraid of summer heat.
You must take good care of your mistress dear
Lest she be chilled by autumn drear.
My dear young mistress, I am going to prepare medicine for you.

Belle (sighing): I know that lovesickness can't be cured by needles of gold,
Nor is there remedy against amorous cold,
Thank you for coming to see me.
A short-lived student cannot fight her destiny.

Together: A patient should not be alarmed.
Take a rest or you would be harmed.

Belle: Dear Master, excuse me for I cannot see you off at the door. By the way, have you calculated the eight words for my destiny?

Chen: Judging from the eight words, you will get better by the Mid-Autumn Day.

But the eight words should be read and reread.
No doctor could revive the dead. (Exit.)

Epilogue of the Scene

Fragrant: How can I bear your frowning brow!
Nun: Useless to pray the Taoist now.
Belle: I am not like a red flower.
Together: East wind, don't blow into our bower!

(Exeunt.)

Scene 3 Untimely Death

(Enter Fragrant Spring.)

Fragrant (Singing to the tune of ***Golden Ornament***):

All the night long the wind and rain
Left my young mistress in pain.
No remedy nor medicine
Could cure her grown so thin.
If she could smile and frown,
She might reap what is sown.
Now she can't frown nor smile.
Could she last a long while?

I have been waiting on my young mistress ill from spring to autumn. Today falls the Mid-Autumn Festival. It is still raining and the wind is dreary. My young mistress' illness seems to get worse. I will try to help her to forget her illness (Singing):

The autumn moon is often veiled in rain;
The flame of her life flickers in vain. (Exit)

(Enter Belle supported by Fragrant)

Fragrant (Singing to the tune of **Fairy of the Magpie Bridge**):

Viewing the moon from empty hall,
I see but cloud on cloud veil all.
Feeling cold, I'm afraid
Into a dream autumn would fade.
What as painful as lovesickness appears?

Only a broken heart's sad tears.

Belle: My pillow can hear the water clock melt away:

So ill, so dull I seem near the end of my day.

The rain is drunken with fragrance of night;

I've grown so thin as to hold chilly autumn in fright.

Fragrant, I am so ill that I do not know what day is today.

Fragrant: Today is the Mid-Autumn Festival.

Belle: Ah! The Festival comes so soon. My father and mother are so worried for me that I am afraid they may not have the mind to enjoy the day.

Fragrant: They would not care.

Belle: Master Chen foretold that I might get better after the Mid-Autumn Festival. Now my illness has not passed away, but turned more severe. Tonight I feel worse than ever. Will you open the window for me to feast my eyes on the beauty of the moon?

(Fragrant opens the window and Belle takes a look.)

(Singing to the tune of ***Talents Gathered Together***):

I ask from which part of the boundless sky

Rises the icy moon so high.

Who would make medicine

For the Moon Goddess so thin?

Why should the west wind blow away

My dream, of which no trace could stay?

How could I meet my love again?

Could he be an immortal to give me pain?

Otherwise how

Could he make me knit my brow?

How could the grief

Gnaw at my heart beyond belief?
(Belle sunk in sullen mood)

Fragrant (Singing to the previous tune):

Why should the departed spring leave but empty dreams?
Why is the veil of mist not replaced by moonbeams?
Life is so dear under the sky:
I thought she would get better by and by.
How could I know she would begin
To grow so thin?
For whom is she pining away?
How could she forsake the beauty of the day?

Let me not tell her the truth. My dear young mistress, the rising moon shines in the sky, and peeps at your bed. Will it not break your sweet dream?

Belle (Gazing at the moon and sighing):

"I long for the Mid-Autumn Day to enjoy my fill.
Now comes the day, but I can't have my will.
The lonely moon shines bright on me in vain;
My life may pass away tonight in wind and rain."
(Singing to the previous tune):
The autumn moon is bright, but not for me.
Shivering in wind, I'm like a leaf of plane tree.
Bony and thin, my illness grows severe;
Hurrying back, I'm like a lonely swan so drear.
Chilled crickets chirp amid the grass.
The paper on my window flutters, alas!
(Startled, she faints away.)
How can I stand

My cold or move my leg or hand!

Fragrant (Shocked): My young mistress faints away with cold.

Madame, will you please come here.

(Enter Zhen.)

Zhen (Singing): I have no worry with my husband's wealth,

But what can I do with my daughter's poor health?

My dear daughter, are you getting better now?

Fragrant: Madame, she is not getting better.

Zhen: How? What can I do?

(Singing to the previous tune):

Since her last visit to the garden in the rear,

She has not been wide awake nor quite clear.

Always sleepy, she cannot raise her heavy head.

Oh! if to a good husband she could be wed!

She would not be a lonely swan by night,

Nor a young phoenix laden with fright.

Could she be on the mend?

I fear it's near her end.

Belle (Coming to her senses and singing to the tune of ***Warbling Orioles***):

What could restore my fleeing spirit to its cell?

Is it the west wind tinkling the iron bell?

(Sobbing) Oh, my dear mom! How much do I owe you!

(Falling on her knees:)

Since my young days, you regard me dearer than gold.

But I cannot be filial now that you are old

O dear mom, it is fate.

In this life I am a flower blossoming in vain.

I only wish to have another life to serve you again.

Together (Sobbing): It is the west wind that we hate,

For it makes red flowers and green leaves desolate.

Zhen (Singing to the previous tune):

Having no sons. we love our daughter fair and wise,

Her pleasing looks and smiling eyes,

How could we bear her to leave her parents dear,

And make us sad and drear!

She would leave empty the month and year.

I think it better to leave this behind

And let nothing trouble and disturb her mind.

Together (sobbing): It is the west wind we hate.

For it makes red flowers and green leaves desolate.

Belle: Dear mom, what if such misfortune should befall me?

Zhen: We might send your remains to our homeland, my dear.

Belle (Sobbing and singing to the tune of ***Jade Oriole***):

How could my coffin go the way

To our homeland so far away!

Zhen: No matter how far, you should go home.

Belle: May I ask a last favor of you, dear mom? There is a mume tree in the back garden which I love best. I would be content to be buried beneath it.

Zhen: Why should you prefer the mume tree?

Belle: Unable to be the Moon Goddess from death free,

I wish to be accompanied by the mume tree.

Zhen (Weeping): Seeing her drowned in sweat and tears,

I would die before that day nears.

Together: We hate the moonlit sky sending wind and showers

To destroy delicate flowers.

Zhen: I should consult with your father.

If medicine could cure,
We'd grudge no money, to be sure. (Exit.)

Belle: Fragrant, do you think I could revive?
(Sighing and singing to the previous tune):
Since young, you have well played your part,
You know what is deep in my heart.
Fragrant, you should serve my parents as you serve me.

Fragrant: You need not tell me that.

Belle: There is one thing I forgot to tell you. My portrait with a verse on it should not be shown to outsiders. After my burial, you should hide it in a sandalwood box and put it amid the lakeside rock.

Fragrant: What for?

Belle: If my dream lover's heart and mine beat as one,
To my innermost call he would run.

Fragrant: Why not defy the misfortune and get married? You may ask our lord and lady to marry the dreamer of mume or willow. What joy for you to live and die together with him!

Belle: I am afraid I cannot wait so long. Alas! alas!
(Fainting away.)

Fragrant: Help! Help! My lord, my lady!
(Enter Du and Zhen)

Du and Zhen (Singing to the tune of ***Orioles Recalled***):
The drum beats at midnight;
We're in a gloomy plight.
The cold rain beating on the window darkens lamplight;
The maid announces our disaster at its height.

Fragrant (Weeping): My young mistress! my dear mistress!

Du and Zhen(Weeping): Dear child!
How can you pass away,

Leaving your dad and mom halfway!
Who would take care of us at the end of our day!

Together: Oh! what regret to see the shade
Of duckweed on the waves should fade!
How can we bear the gale destroy lotus of jade!

Belle (Coming back to her senses.)

Du: Wake up, my dear! Here is your dad.

Belle (Looking at Du): **Ah! dad, will you please help me to the hall?**

Du: Here is my arm, my dear child. (Offering his right arm.)

Belle (Singing to the tune of ***Epilogue***):
I fear the flowers on the trees
Should fall before the morning breeze.
Would you set up a stone tablet at my young grave
To recall what my broken heart would crave?
Dad, is it Mid-Autumn Festival tonight?

Du: Yes, my dear child.

Belle: It has rained all night long.
How could the setting moon rerise!
(Sighing) When the breeze utters sighs,
Have you heard flowers sing their farewell song?

(Exeunt.)

Epilogue of the Scene

Du: Your soul goes back to Yellow Spring so deep.

Zhen: After a life of eighteen long, long years.

Fragrant: Our heart would break when we call you and weep.

Together: Thinking of you, our sorrow reappears.

(Exeunt.)

Scene 4 The Infernal Judge

(Enter the infernal judge, followed by the soul of Belle.)

Judge (Singing to the tune of ***Cherubic Song***):

With rosy cheeks so tender
And waist so slender,
Were you while alive as fair as a flower,
Or a companion in a drinking hour?
With a hairpin slanting in the air,
Were you a songstress fair
Or a dancer beyond compare?
A smile hangs on your face,
Where was your dwelling place?
How could you have so much grace?
Of what illness did you die?
Were you from a family ranking high?
Your color looked unlike infernal dye.

Belle's Soul: I am not wed,

Nor drunken dead.
But only naturally rosy and red,
I dreamed of a young scholar asking me
To write a verse in praise of the willow tree.
He was so passionate
That when awake, I could not but meditate
What to write. Then two lines appear:

"If the Moon Goddess be a bride,
She would stand by the willow's side."
I felt so sad and drear,
No to find my dear.

Judge: Are you not lying? How could lovesickness kill?
(Singing to the tune of ***Magpie on the Branch***):
You are so young a maiden fair.
How can you trust in dreaming affair?
Of dreams come true I've never heard,
Nor fortune told by splitting word.
Oh! How could a scholar win
Your heart? How could a dream be trusted in?

Belle's Soul: I dare not say how winning is he.
I only woke to see a flower fall on me.

Judge: Send for the floral fairy of the Nan'an Prefectural garden.
(Enter the Floral Fairy at call.)

Fairy (Singing): Spring wanes, with rosy rain falling in showers.
The mountain fragrant with songs of falling flowers,
Salute, Your Lordship. (Saluting him)

Judge: Floral Fairy, this maiden's soul said that she died when startled awake from her dream by a falling flower in the back garden of Nan'an Prefecture. Was it true?

Fairy: It was true. While dreaming of a tryst with a young scholar in the prefectural garden. She was startled by the fall of a flower and died of lovesickness.

Judge: Were you transformed into a young scholar to seduce this fair maiden?

Fairy: What could induce me to seduce her?

Judge: Do you think that we in the infernal world could be fooled by your tales? The maiden died of lovesickness. Let her be transformed into a swallow or an oriole!

Fairy: Your Lordship, this maiden was guilty in a dream as whimsical as the morning breeze or the waning moon. Besides, her father is an upright official who has only one daughter. So will it please Your Lordship to remit her punishment?

Judge (To Belle): Who is your father?

Belle: My father is Du Bao, former prefect of Nan'an County and now promoted to governor of Huaiyang.

Judge: So you are a noble maiden. All right. On account of your father, I shall submit a report to the celestial court and then pass my sentence on you.

Belle: May I ask a favor of Your Lordship to find out the cause of my lovesickness?

Judge: That can be found out in the *Book of Broken Hearts*.

Belle: Would you please do me another favor to find out who is my husband-to-be? Is he called Liu the Dreamer of Willow or Lover of Mume Flower?

Judge: Let me consult the *Book of Marriage*. (Turning aside)Here it is. Liu the Dreamer of Willow or Lover of Mume Flower, who will soon win the laurel crown in the recent civil service examinations. His wife will be Du the Belle, who trysted with him at first and will be married to him in the end. But this should be kept secret.

(Turning around) Yes, there is Liu the Dreamer who will take you to wife. Now I will release you as guiltless. You may leave the infernal town and go with the wind to find Liu the Dreamer.

Fairy (To Belle): You should thank His Lordship for the favor he has shown you.

Belle: Thank Your Lordship for giving me a second life.

(Exeunt.)

Epilogue of the Scene

Fairy: Drunken, I slant my black cap over my hair gray;
Belle: The wonder-working wind won't swell the flag all day.
Judge: I fairly judge human affairs from year to year,
Together: Waiting for Minister Xiao to be my compeer.

ACT V

Scene 1 The Portrait Discovered

(Enter Liu the Dreamer of Mume Flower)

Liu (Singing to the tune of ***Golden Ornament***):

Nothing is more surprising to me than spring.
On my journey, of nothing else do I sing.
My apricot-hued gown was wet with rain,
But the wind dried it up again
Today the weather's fine,
Still there's the cloud's trace on the sunned sheet of mine.
"The courtyard fragrant with pear flowers,
This year for me is full of worrying hours.
I do not know how much grieved is the willow tender,
But I have my waist as the poet's slender."

I lay ill for days in the Mume Blossom Convent. By luck, friend good at medicine cured me. Affected by spring grief recently, where can I go to assuage it? Here comes the old nun of the convent. (Enter the Nun.)

Nun (Singing to the tune of ***A String of Pearls***):

What cannot an old crowned nun find
In a young scholar's mind?
I know why he is fond of day-dreams;
He yawns from sunrise till wane the moonbeams.
How are you, my dear young scholar?

Liu: I am getting better now, but I feel bored with too much leisure. How

could there be no garden and sights to see in such a convent?

Nun: There is a garden at the back of the convent with deserted pavilions and verandas and adorned with various flowers in full bloom. You may go there to pass your leisure. But be not moved by its decay please!

Liu: How could I be?

Nun (Sighing): That is my advice. You may go your way in the western corridor along the painted wall and find the wicket gate a hundred paces away. If you go further in,you will find the poolside pavilion, where you may while away your time without my company.

(Singing): You may enjoy a garden of renown,
But be not moved by its up and down.

Liu: Since there is such a garden, I would go there along the winding way. (Walking.) This must be the western corridor. The wicket gate is green with banana leaves but stands half in ruins. (Sighing and singing):

The balustrade looks as if old,
But the crumbled walls are too sad to behold,
Where is the moon of by gone days with the breeze?
There are only thousands of mist-veiled willow trees.
What a sight the garden must have been!
(Singing to the tune of ***Approaching Good Event***):
The breeze won't blow and the moon shines no more;
West of the painted wall southward opens the door.
(Slipping.) How slippery does the moss grow
Along the crumbled walls high and low!
Why closed is the gate looking like a butterfly?

The garden must have been haunted in days gone by.
See names inscribed on the stems of the bamboo!
It must have been a place of rendezvous.
So many years have passed;
Only their names are left at last.
Then flowers overspread along the path, alas!
The garden now is overgrown with weed and grass.
It is strange the Mume Blossom Convent could provide
Such a garden, so wide.
See the winding stream!
(Singing to the tune of ***Silk-paved Way***):
Within the closed door
There must have been a Peach Blossom Shore.
But now the waterside pavilion lies in decay,
Only painted boats empty stay.
The garden swing can't sway,
It was not destroyed by fire or war.
How can it be in such disorder?
Is the heart-broken owner banished to the border?
If it has nothing to do with a love affair,
How can the lakeside rocks seem built for a pair?

What a lovely rocky hill! (Looking into it.) **Ah! There is a little box between two rocks. I'll lean on the left side to see what it is.** (Taking out the box.) **It is a box of sandalwood.** (Opening the box and looking in.) **Ah! There is a portrait of Benevolent Buddha! What a blessing for me! I will take it to my study and pay my daily homage. It would be better than leaving it unearthed here.** (Singing to the tune of ***A Thousand Autumns***):

Amid the rugged rocks there's a sandalwood box fine.
How could I know it is Benevolent Buddha's shrine?
On the rocky peak at the height
There are stone birds in flight.
The portrait must be the gift for my ancestor old,
I should perfume it over a censer of gold,
And bow to it with my head to the ground
So that the blessing for me might be found.
What do you think of what I say,
And of the homage I will pay?

(Arriving.) **Here I am again in the convent. I will put the portrait in its shrine and choose a day to pay my homage.**

(Enter the nun.)

Nun: Here you are back, Master Liu.

Liu (Singing the ***Epilogue***):

Roaming all day, I have so much regret.
When back to the garden, I'm cold with sweat.
You told me not to be moved.
How could I not for my beloved?

Epilogue of the Scene

Liu: Secluded, near the woods with fountain I would stay.
Nun: You would be grieved to dream of a rainy spring day.
Liu: Where can I hang the portrait in the hall?
Together: In face of three peaks greened when Flowers fall.

(Exeunt.)

Scene 2 The Portrait Admired

(Enter Liu the Dreamer of Mume Flower.)

Liu (Singing): Palm leaves cannot retain rain drops;

On peony tips the breeze stops.

A half clear sketch arrests the eye

On my way to Spring with head high.

Lonely and bored, I passed my leisure in the garden where I found a box in which there is a picture which looks like Benevolent Buddha. I could not appreciate it in rainy days. Today the weather turns fine, I'll open the box and take out the picture for appreciation.

(Taking out the box and spreading out the scroll.)

(Singing to the tune of ***Golden Oriole***):

Autumn casts shade

On the River of Stars which fade.

Buddha displays his face

With so much grace.

His person dignified

Would appear by seaside. (Meditating.)

Why should he have left his image divine

In lotus-furnished shrine?

How could these tiny feet

Treading on waves become so fleet?

Is it the image of Buddha we adore?

Let me contemplate it once more.
(Singing to the slow tune of ***the Gallant Cadet***):
I have got it. If my guess is right.
The portrait hanging in my hall may be
That of the Goddess of the Moon bright.
So elegant and graceful is she!
If it is the goddess I adore,
I'd pay her homage all the more.
I'd ask her if the laurel crown will belong to me.
Why is there no cloud under her feet?
Why by her side no laurel sweet?
If it's nor Buddha nor Moon Goddess fair,
How can an earthly beauty be beyond compare?
I am surprised
To find someone I seem to have recognized
I try to ask my heart
If it's the work done by a painter's art,
Or is it drawn by the hand
Of the beauty herself of this land?
(Singing to the tune of ***Overture of Warbling Oriole***):
I ask the portrait where comes the maiden fair,
To Beauty's shadow cast in moonlight it's a pair,
Before such a fair maiden's brow,
How could all flowers not bow?
Her natural grace beyond fancy flies.
Who could see through vernal cloud with his eyes?
How could a painter come to her so near?
The painter must be herself, maiden dear.

Wait a minute. There are a few lines on the scroll.

(Looking) **It is a quatrain. I'll read it.**

(Reading): The portrait seems alive when viewed nearby;
Viewed from afar, a fairy seems to fly.
If I might be the laurel winner's bride,
It must be by the mume's or willow's side.

Ah! It is a picture of a fair maiden enjoying pleasure. Why should the poet mention mume or willow? It seems strange.

(Singing to the tune of ***Talents Gathered Together***):

Behold! The mountain overgrown with mumes bar the sky.
How could the poet know I would come by?
If I could win the laurel crown,
What a delight! I would loiter here up and down.
How could the goddess know my name?
How could she know my flame?
Have I met her in dreams?
My heart's upset, it seems.

(Singing to the tune of ***Golden Oriole***):

The maiden fair
Comes from the air.
Her wide-spread sleeves
Sway like fallen leaves.
Her silk skirt trails
Like phoenix' tails.
Her eyebrows knit apart
Reveal her locked Vernal heart.
Green hills extend
And melt the mist in the farthest end,

Between our eyes waves flow.
What is the secret message? Who can know?
A green mume in her hand,
Could I in its place stand?
(Singing to the tune of ***Overture of Warbling Oriole***):
You read your verse, green mume in hand;
My heart palpitating, here I stand.
I cannot stay my hunger by a portrait fair.
Nor can you quench your thirst by a shower in air.
My dear maiden, you are the lotus leaf in bloom,
Smiling with rosy lips in gloom.
What have your speaking eyes to say?
You only need the breath to come to see the day.
You can draw a picture so fine
And write poetic line.
With you before the eye,
How can I not write a verse in reply?
For picture shows your talent high —
An earthly painter from the sky,
Of laurel crown if I have the pride,
Spring would come to my willow's side.
(Singing to the tune of ***Royal Forest***):
She can paint pictures and write
Lines in reply to verses bright,
If I see her appear,
I would call her my beauty dear,
And cry till blood blend with tear,
Till she comes down in flight,

And treads on waves with steps light.
Where can I find her? I'm lonely here.
Before her portrait, early or late,
I can only prostrate,
Admire and appreciate.
(Singing the ***Epilogue***):
Finding the picture of a dreamed mate,
What can I do but felicitate?
There's something to do with willow or mume flower,
Oh! my dear, could your person come into my bower?

Epilogue of the Scene

Do not complain of the portrait at all,
But hang it and admire it in the hall.
Take hint from the willow you hear her sing!
You would not wake up, drunk in dreams of spring.

(Exit.)

Scene 3 The Roving Soul

(Enter Belle's Soul with her face half covered with her sleeve.)

Belle's Soul (Singing to the tune of ***Knotweed Flower***):

Coming down from the Homesick Tower as in dreams,
Night quivers and gleams with starry beams.
In the graveyard deep silence reigns at dead of night.
(Startled by a dog's bark in the dark)
Only a dog barks in starlight.
Flowers in bloom
Sway in the gloom.
A chilly night,
The pear tree casts the shadow of its blossoms white.
Turning around the pavilion of peony red,
I can still find the rose bed.
Since my parents left, three years have passed away.
(Sobbing) I'm grieved at crumbled wall and deserted pathway.
What is in sight?
Flickering green lamplight,
(Listening): From where comes human voice?
(Singing to the lengthened tune of ***Lament of a Fair Lady***):
Daughter of noble family in bygone days,
Now fallen flower on running water flowing away,
A fair maiden would linger and delay,
What can I say?

By nature I will do what I like to.
Tonight I see before me one star or two.
We live for love and die for love too.
Without love, what can we do?

I am the Soul of Du Belle. I died of lovesickness in a dream. As the tenth Infernal Judge was removed from office, none would look into my case, and I was imprisoned for three years. As luck would have it, the newly appointed judge is sympathetic and gives me leave to revisit this land. Now the moon is bright and the breeze soft, Why don't I go back to the garden? Here it is the back yard of my former study. How can it be turned into a convent, to my disappointment?

(Singing to the tune of ***Red Peach Blossoms***):

Awake from drunk dreams, a broken heart appears.
Who could bring back my unlived years?
A soul may rove companionless.
I would appear in decent dress,
Followed by my shadow in view.
The breeze brings down the dew.
Clouds veil the Plough afar,
The moon attracts the star.
So I'm attracted by this sight,
When flowers' shadows sway in early night.

(Tinkling sound heard from within.)

What makes my heart feel not at ease?
It is the bells ringing in the breeze.

(Singing to the tune of ***Tiger Coming down from the Mountain***):

I hear calls coming from afar,

Let me listen what they are.

Voice within: My beauty dear, my sister dear!

Belle: Who is calling? Whom is he calling? Let me listen again.

Voice within: My beauty dear, my sister dear!

Belle (Sighing and singing to the tune of ***Drunken Lover's Return***):

Lonely I lived; lonely I die.
A lover calls; the beloved won't reply.
Why don't you call the name
Of your dear flame?
So lonely is my soul:
Who would reply my verse on the scroll?
I don't know who will be my mate;
I cannot stop but wait.

(Calls repeated within.)

Is it the call of my dear scholar? It seems
To be a talk in dreams.

(Singing to the tune of ***Black Frog***):

Even the heartless would smile with amorous eye.
How could I not echo twice or thrice in reply?
From my dreaming eyes drop by drop fall cold bloodlike tears.
Could it be the Dreamer of Willow or Mume who appears?
I still remember the waterside towers
Bathed in moonlight and soft breeze amid flowers,
My soul then on the wing may find before
A blessed night of three stars or four.
The Plough barring the sky will usher in the day.
So I cannot longer stay.

(Exit.)

Scene 4 The Tryst

(Enter Liu the Dreamer of Mume Flower.)

Liu (Singing to the tune of ***Night Sailing Boat***):

Where can I find the celestial beauty of this land?
Her shadow floats like moonlight over the sand.
I linger long with deep regret,
Thinking of her I can't forget.
Beyond the western hills the sun has set.
A rosy cloud sails down from the blue sky;
The flowerlike beauty smiles with beaming eyes.
On whom is drawn this picture of a fair face?
For me she reveals unspeakable grace.

Since I saw the beauty's portrait, I have been longing to see her person day and night. When night is deep, I would read her pearl like verse and read into her heart. If I could meet her in dreams, I would be happy as caressed by the vernal breeze. Behold, how beautiful she is! Her heart would speak through her lips and ripple in her eyes just as:

"The rosy cloud and lonely swan together fly,
The autumn water blends with the azure sky."

(Singing to the tune of ***Fragrance All Over***):

The evening breeze swaying peach blossoms blows
A wreath of rosy cloud down on the stream which flows
And would allure

A beauty elegant, graceful and pure.
Before the newly crimson-gauzed window bright
Her fair portrait enchants my heart and sight.
My beauty dear, my sister dear in view,
How much I am lovesick for you!
(Singing to the tune of ***Idly Pencilled Eyebrows***):
The noble maiden is so delicate and shy,
She must be daughter of official ranking high.
She looks into the glass with amorous heart
And draws a picture of her vernal face with art.
Has she ever anticipated
That I who find it would be fascinated?
(Singing to the tune of ***Plane Tree***):
I see her portrait like the moon descend;
It makes me lovesick without end.
I used to sleep in face of the moon bright,
But now from night to night
Her dazzling light
Bewilders my heart and sight
On a night still
And so tranquil.
Day and night I gaze at her face,
I would hold her in my embrace,
If it won't spoil the scroll.
Am I playing my role? I'll read her verse once more.
(Reading the verse.)
(Singing to the tune of ***Silk-washing Stream***):
A verse should be read to an understanding heart.

Does mume or willow in your verse play a part?
Your love bursts into lakeside flower with leaves green,
Turned into a fairy flying on the screen.
What can I do but prostrate
Before you? But I hesitate.
What troubles your heart, knits your brows and blushes your face?
Do you not know your lover is in a nearby place?
My beauty dear, my sister dear, would you please
Allow me to caress you as moonlight or breeze?
(Singing to the tune of ***A Gallant's Cap***):
If you can paint a pair of lovers on a scroll,
Then of the reed beside a jade I'd play the role.
My beauty dear, my sister dear,
Your cloudlike hair has screened your crescent-like ear.
Of my lovesickness can it hear?
(Singing to the tune of ***the Autumn Moon***):
Too funny am I who
Wish a dream to come true,
To catch the moon hanging over the cloud in the sky,
The shadow greening the forest in the mountain high.
But you are a far-off star
Only to be admired from afar.
(Singing to the tune of ***the Eastern Mountain***):
If I chant magic spell,
I could move stone statue well.
If I preach the creed,
I would rain flower and reed.
Why can't I move the goddess fair

To come down from the air?

(Putting hands on the scroll on hearing the roaring wind.)

I can't but seize

Hold of this scroll lest it be blown off by the breeze.

I had better find another master painter to make a copy of this picture lest it be spoiled by the wind.

(Singing to the tune of ***Golden Lotus***):

Am I talking of the goddess in vain?

How could I pray her to come down and to remain?

If somewhere with her I could meet,

I would see how could she be so sweet.

And I'd compare

Her breeze-caressed face with her image fair.

Let me trim the wick and have a closer look!

(Singing to the tune of ***Semi-epilogue***):

Could such a beauty be true and live still?

(The wind blows and the flame flickers.)

Oh, the wind is so chill,

Afraid its sparks might spoil the portrait from above,

I'll close the window to sleep and dream of my love.

(Sleeping.)

(Enter Du Belle's Soul.)

Belle: My dream cannot come true in the underground night,

How could I pay my lover's debt of days gone by?

My soul tries to find my portrait, led by moonlight,

In the breeze I can only utter sigh on sigh.

I am the Soul of Du Belle, who died of lovesickness after a dream in the peony garden. While alive, I drew a picture of my

own image and hid it in the crevice of the lakeside rock. On the scroll I wrote the following verse:

If I might be the laurel winner's bride,
It must be by the mume's or willow's side.

When my soul revisited the garden, I heard in the east chamber a scholar call in low voice: "My beauty dear, my sister dear!" His voice, though low, yet laden with grief, was so plaintive that it stirred my heart. Silent, I entered his room and found a picture hanging on the wall. It was nothing other than the portrait I drew of myself, with an additional poem on it in reply to mine, written by Liu the Dreamer of Willow. As I was predestined to be the laurel winner's bride, so I told the Infernal Judge, who was kind enough to allow me to realize my dream and pass the night with him. (Singing to the tune of ***Idle Homage***):

I am afraid
My powder and fragrance would fade.
My crimson silk sleeves stained with tears,
My lover in moonlight appears.
Turning my head,
I find my hair dishevelled.
Ah, behold, his room is ahead!
I don't know if it is Peach Blossom shore.
I shall inquire while going on before.

Liu (Reciting Belle's verse):

If I could be the laurel winner's bride,
It must be by the mume's or willow's side.

Ah, my dear beauty, my dear sister!

Belle (Saddened while listening, and singing to the previous tune):

His love call makes me shed tears.

He recites my verse and no mistake appears.

Has he not yet gone to bed?

Liu (Calling again): My dear beauty, my dear sister!

Belle: Oh, he is reciting in his dream.

Do not make noise

But listen to his voice!

I'll knock at his window screen

Made of bamboo green. (Knocking.)

Liu (Startled): My dear beauty, my dear sister!

Belle (Grieved): Let my soul go nearer to him.

Liu: Who is knocking at my window screen? Is it a man or just the breeze?

Belle: All, open please!

Liu: Who would come so late into the night? Is it the old nun of the convent sending tea to me? If it is, I would thank her very much, but I do not want to drink now.

Belle: It is me.

Liu: Are you the young nun?

Belle: No.

Liu: It is strange that you are neither the old nor the young nun. I shall open the door to see who you are. (Opening he door.)

(Singing to the tune of ***Playing with the Fairy Lamp***):

From where comes such a maiden nice,

Charming to my surprise?

Belle (Slipping in before Liu closes the door, adjusting her dress and saluting): Dear Master, Boundless blessing to you!

Liu: Welcome, welcome! my fair maiden! May I ask you where you are coming from? And why are you coming so late?

Belle: Just make a guess, dear Master!

Liu (Singing to the tune of ***Red Winter Coat***):

Are you the Weaving Maid from the Milky Way afar?
Or her waiting maid eloping with the morning star?

Belle: They are immortals in Heaven. How could they descend on earth?

Liu: Are you following the crow as a phoenix free?

Belle (Waving her head.)

Liu: Is your lover's steed tethered to the willow tree?

Belle: I have never seen my love face to face.

Liu: Going to Peach Blossom Fountain, you have lost your way,
Or eloping with your gallant, you go astray?

Belle: I am neither.

Liu: Why will your rosy sleeves share my window's green light?
How dare you go alone so late into the night?

Belle (Singing to the previous tune):

I am not the fairy from the sky to strew flowers,
Nor to share your window's light in reading hours,
I am unlike the faithless Flying Swallow Queen,
Nor the new widow eloping with the talent unseen,
My dear Master, have you ever dreamed like a butterfly to be bewildered and bewitched on a flower?

Liu: Yes, I have.

Belle: So have I. In my dream, I flew on the wing of oriole's song to the willow's home. If you ask me where my home is, it is a few doors from yours.

Liu (Thinking): Oh yes, I saw you once strolling in the west garden at sunset.

Belle: It was me,

Liu: With whom are you living in your family?

Belle (Singing to the tune of ***Vernal Song***):

Between the setting sun
And fragrant grass a lonely one
Like me lives with no other
Than her father and mother.
I am sixteen,
A virgin flower with leaves green.
My heart was stirred by vernal breeze
When I saw how you stood and moved with ease.
I come here only to keep your company at night
That we may have heart-to-heart talk by candlelight.

Liu (Turning aside): It is midnight. How can it be possible for such a beauty as bright as the full moon or pearl to favor me with a visit so late in the night? What shall I do?

(Singing to the previous tune):

You are so wonderfully bright and fair;
Your beauty is beyond compare.
Your smile would turn into silver the candlelight,
I'd ask the River of Stars what night is tonight,
How could such a jade like beauty overhead
Come down on earth to share my bed? (Turning aside.)
Could she be a fair maiden of noble family
Coming to make fun of me? (Turning back.)

How could you favor me with a visit so late into the night?
I am afraid it is only a dream.

Belle (Smiling): It is not a dream but a fact, and I do not know if you will accept me.

Liu: I am afraid it is not true for I dare not believe such a beauty as you would not reject such a poor scholar as me. So how can I not accept you?

Belle: Well, you are exactly what I expect to be. (Singing to the tune of ***Playing the Old***):

Deep is the vale and out of sight,
You hastened my early flower to bloom at night.
In marriage I have never been a part;
You know it is in your heart.
I am raised by a noble family,
But in the Pavilion of Peony
I first knew love
With you above
And with the lakeside rocks near by.
How I felt shy!
Now by your window screen
The breeze whispers unseen.
Far better than tea-drinking night,
We may enjoy the priceless breeze and the moon bright.

Liu (Singing to the tune of ***Drop by Drop in Gold***):

Startled from dreams,
I wake to find chilly moonbeams.
The moon's so bright,
I wonder if the goddess comes down from Witch Height.
How could you pass the shade
Without being afraid?
How could you descend on the moss
Without slippery and loss?

How could you escape your parent's eyes
Without care for their sighs?
How could you find my room
Without mistake or fear of gloom.
You see the Dipper hanging low,
Asleep the flowers go,
While we enjoy our fill
And read verse as we will.
We have outdone the moon and breeze
When I caress you tenderly as we please.
How much do I owe you?
Half of our bliss to you is due.

Belle: Excuse me, I have something to tell you.

Liu: Why should you be so polite? You may just say what you will.

Belle: I have given you all I have, heart and soul. I hope you will do the same. Do not change your mind. From tonight on, I will come to share your pillow, and so my wish is fulfilled.

Liu (Smiling): You have done me so much good. How could I forget you?

Belle: Still I have something else to say. Please allow me to go back before cockcrow, and do not see me off for fear of the morning chill.

Liu: I will do all you ask me to. May I ask you a question? What is your name?

Belle (Singing to the tune of ***Endless Love***):

Flowers have roots, so has the jade.
My root would arouse gossip, I am afraid.

Liu:I hope you will come from night to night.

Belle: Dear Master,

Let us be the first flowers blooming bright.

Epilogue of the Scene

Liu: Such beauty in such ecstasy has never been met.
Belle: The moonlit bower at midnight, could we forget?
Your cloud bringing me fresh shower is hard to seek.
Liu: The fairy queen flies down from on high from which peak?

Scene 5 The Next Tryst

(Enter Liu the Dreamer of Mume Flower.)

Liu (Singing to the tune of ***Washerwoman's Song***):

The water-clock announces midnight:
On mid-court the moon sheds her light.
Is incense lit and prayer read?
Each inch of incense burnt is scarlet red.
Your fingers look like bamboo shoots so slender;
A beauty's face
So full of grace
May change a scholar's heart so tender,

I am Liu the Dreamer of Mume Flower, a student devoted to studies coming to Nan'an on my way to the capital. I have the sheer luck of being visited by a beauty of the neighborhood, who smiled so sweet and allowed me to bring fresh shower to her virgin flower, and who came late in the night and went early with the morning breeze. I do not know when she will come tonight.

If her lotus feet move an inch their step light,
An inch would be burned of the silver candle bright.

But when she comes. I must welcome her in high spirit. So why don't I doze off a while before she comes? (Dozing.)

(Enter the Soul of Du Belle.)

Belle (Singing to the tune of ***The Heart Pleased***):

I struggle on my way;

Though dead, my heart still goes astray.
How could I do wrong to my scholar bright
By letting him sit idly by candlelight?
(Entering the room.)
I find him sitting there asleep,
Uncovered though spring is chilly when night is deep.
What is he doing but waiting for me?
Let me wake him up with glee! My dear Master!

Liu (Waking up): **My dear sister! Excuse me for my negligence.**
I will adjust my dress and come out to welcome you,
But I'm afraid of windy night and chilly dew.
I fear the flower will fall asleep
When night is deep.

Belle: My dear Master, it's hard for me to pass the lonely night,
So I would come and sit with you by candlelight.

Liu: How could you come with such light pace?

Belle: I would not raise dust nor leave trace.

Liu: I think of you by day and dream of you by night.

Belle: Coming to your window, I find you asleep.

Liu: I am only waiting for you in my heart deep.
My dear sister, why are you late tonight?

Belle (Singing to the tune of ***Embroidered Belt***):
Be not annoyed for my coming late.
How could I forget my dear mate?
Before the incense is lit,
How could I my parents quit?
After I put my needlework aside
By my bedside,

I left my room in haste,

Only with golden rings around my waist.

I come without powdering my face,

In simple dress with simple grace.

Liu: Thank you, my love. But without wine, how to pass the night blessed?

Belle: I forgot to tell you, I have brought a pot of wine with flower and fruit and left them on the balustrade. Let mp go and fetch them to pass this fine night.

(Going out and reentering with wine, flower and fruit.)

Liu: My hearty thanks! Will you please tell me what fruit it is?

Belle: Green mumes.

Liu: And what flower?

Belle: Beautiful canna flower.

Liu: I am so green a hand as the mume fruit while you are as beautiful as the canna flower. Let us drink together a cup of wine! (They drink from the same cup.)

Belle (Singing to the tune of ***White Silk***):

Fill the golden cup with sweet wine!

Liu: Brew in your vernal heart waves of jade fine!

Tipsy, what is there I have to dread?

Where blows the eastern breeze, leaves are green and flowers red.

Belle: There is no fruit or flower rare.

See the mume fruit and canna flower there!

Do you not know we love the heart of the fruit

And the flower with its root?

Liu (Singing to the tune of ***Drunken in Time of Peace***):

The mume fruit is small,

The fruit like a languid beauty in the hall.

The mume is sentimental,
Into the flower's open heart it will fall.
The mume brings juice in shower
All the night long for the thirsting flower,
The joy is hard to seek:
You smile with dimple on the cheek
I rain my kisses on your lips;
The mume's juice on your green waves drips.
The canna flower turns red
With its leaves outspread.
The mume no longer sour
Turns into a sweet flower.

Belle (Singing to the tune of ***White Silk***):

How lively heaves my breast!
For the moon and the breeze it's a paradise blest.
Last night behind the silken screen in the dim shade.
How can I forget the strong love with me you made?
Why should we whisper more
Than in our tryst before?

Liu: Let us sink into a sound sleep!

Belle: How bright is the moon in night deep!
Let us sit for a longer while
In face of the Moon Goddess' smile!
If she is not jealous of me,
We should be a company of happy three.

(Note) Liu the Dreamer of Mume Flower and the Soul of Du Belle

make a vow that they would be man and wife when she comes to life. After her revival, she is married to Liu, who wins the laurel crown at the civil service examinations in the end.

许译中国经典诗文集

牡丹亭

【明】汤显祖 著

许渊冲 许明 译

五洲传播出版社 中华书局

序

中国历史上有四大古典诗剧：元代的《西厢记》，明代的《牡丹亭》，清代的《长生殿》和《桃花扇》。《西厢记》写爱情和封建思想的矛盾，《牡丹亭》更进一步，写爱情的生死斗争。如果说《西厢记》中爱情战胜了父母之命的封建思想，那么，《牡丹亭》中杜丽娘还魂，起死回生，可以说是爱情战胜了死亡。和这四大诗剧差不多同时，西方有莎士比亚的历史悲剧可以和中国的古典诗剧先后媲美。一般说来，《西厢记》写张生和莺莺的爱情，舞台本到第四折的“草桥惊梦”为止，以情人的生离作结。莎剧《罗密欧与朱丽叶》比《西厢记》约晚一二百年，写罗朱的青春恋和家族的矛盾，以情人的死别作结。生离死别，都是人生悲剧。但《西厢记》五折本以张生和莺莺的婚配结束，说明古代中国人对大团圆的爱好；莎剧却写情人的死亡化解了家族的矛盾，显示了以理化情的趋势，从中可以看出中西文化发展的不同。《牡丹亭》的作者汤显祖和莎士比亚是同代人，《牡丹亭》是他的代表作。而莎士比亚的代表作是《哈姆雷特》，两个剧本是否可以比较呢？这点下面再谈。《长生殿》写唐玄宗和杨贵妃的爱情影响了唐代的兴衰，而莎剧《安东尼和克莉奥佩特拉》写不爱江山爱美人的罗马大将和埃及女王的恋情与斗争，都是用历史来说明“玉颜自古关兴废”的哲学思想。最后，《桃花扇》通过一个文人的感情生活和政治斗争来反映明朝灭亡的历史现实，在莎剧中似乎没有可比较的，只有《李尔王》中的国王因为轻信甜言蜜语而失去了江山，也许可以和明朝的末代皇帝相提并论罢。

现在再看《牡丹亭》和《哈姆雷特》，是不是有可以比较的呢？莎剧以父王显灵开始，引起了王子的疑心，于是用假戏演真事，求得了真与假的统一，思想上也引起了生和死、爱和恨的斗争：是为父王复仇呢？还是为了母爱而忍气吞声呢？总的看来，悲剧中隐含着西方戏剧中光荣与爱情的斗争，也就是情与理的矛盾。而《牡丹亭》呢，剧中死去的不是父王，而是活着的杜丽娘；剧中也有生和死的冲突，但不是为死者复仇，而是向生者求爱，为爱情而死的问题。莎剧中也有爱情的插曲，如哈姆雷特对奥菲莉娅的爱情，但爱情和理性有矛盾，结果是理性战胜了爱情。《牡丹亭》却相反，是爱情战胜了理性，使梦想变成了现实，甚至把以理释情的《诗经·关雎》也恢复了情爱的本来面目。

莎剧中最著名的一段是哈姆雷特的独白，下面是卞之琳的译文：

“活下去还是不活，这是问题。
要做到高贵，究竟该忍气吞声
来容受狂暴的命运矢石交攻呢，
还是该挺身反抗无边的苦恼，
扫他个干净？……”

“活下去”应该是为了复仇，“不活”自然是无可奈何了。“要做到高贵”不可能是“忍气吞声”，“狂暴的命运”是指叔父弑君夺位，母后受骗再嫁。如果叔父是“矢”，那母后就是“石”，两人就是“矢石交攻”了。至于“挺身反抗”自然是指为父报仇。“无边的苦恼”是指阴谋和欺骗。如要高贵，自然要揭发阴谋和欺骗，然后“打扫干净”。但是揭发要有证据，父王显灵不足为凭。复仇是情感问题，证据是理智问题，这就产生了情和理的矛盾斗争。

《牡丹亭》中的情理矛盾，体现在女主角杜丽娘身上，却出现在她的老师陈最良的唱词和她的丫鬟春香的说白之中。如陈最良在第二本第二出《闺塾》的《掉角儿》中唱道：

“论六经，《诗经》最葩，闺门内许多风雅：
有指证，姜嫄产哇；不嫉妒，后妃贤达……
有风有化，宜室宜家……
《诗》三百，一言以蔽之，
没多些，只‘无邪’两字，付与儿家。”

这是说理。至于言情，则作者在第二本第三出中借春香之口说：小姐

“读到《毛诗》第一章：‘窈窕淑女，君子好逑。’
悄然废书而叹曰：‘圣人之情，尽见于此矣。
今古同怀，岂不然乎？’……小姐说：‘关了的雎鸠，
尚然有洲渚之兴，可以人而不如鸟乎？’”

在第二本第四出《惊梦》中，小姐又说：

“天呵，春色恼人，信有之乎！常观诗词乐府，
古之女子，因春感情，遇秋成恨，诚不谬矣。
吾今年已二八，未逢折桂之夫，忽慕春情，
怎得蟾宫之客？”

这就是情了。不过《牡丹亭》在杜府中只有女主角和丫鬟重情，父母老师都更重理，情理的矛盾表现在父女、母女、师生之间，是外在的，所以比较简单。而《哈姆雷特》的矛盾，从上面的独白看来却主要是内心的，所以更加深刻。自然也有外在矛盾，那就是叔侄矛盾、母子矛盾，所以更加错综复杂。因为《牡丹亭》中的父女矛盾，父代表理，女代表情，所以比较简单。而《哈姆雷特》中的叔侄矛盾，叔父本身也有矛盾斗争：内心既不喜欢侄子，表面上又不得不装出喜欢的神气，于是说话就复杂了。如叔侄开始的对话：

叔：得，哈姆雷特，我的侄儿，我的儿……

理智上和情感上都是侄儿，但又不得不装出父子的感情，所以就说"我的儿"。这下哈姆雷特可难办了，情感上不能接受，理智上又不好拒绝，怎么办呢？问题越难回答，越可以看出莎翁的生花妙笔：

侄：亲上加亲；越亲越不相亲！

叔：你怎么还是让愁云惨雾笼罩着你？

侄：陛下，太阳大，受不了这个热劲"儿"。

这个译文之妙，简直可以和原文相比，如"亲上加亲"，"热劲儿"的"儿"字，和叔父说"我的儿"针锋相对，译出了原文的双关意思，又写出了哈姆雷特的怀疑心理。一个"疑"字，是全剧的关键词。《牡丹亭》中也有怀疑，如杜丽娘怀疑《诗经•关雎》写的不是后妃之德，却相信"君子好逑"是"圣人之情"，因信而梦假成真，这和莎剧中的真剧假演，几乎又有异曲同工之妙。丽娘之“信”和王子之“疑”构成了两个剧本不同的剧情，也说明了中西文化发展的不同方向。西方因怀疑而探索求真，发展了科学思想；中方因轻信而求安，发展了保守求稳的心理。所以明朝初年，郑和船队下南洋时，中国国力之强，在全世界首屈一指，但明清交替之后，就逐渐衰退，落后于西方。比较《牡丹亭》和莎剧，也可看出一点根苗。莎剧中哈姆雷特看见父王显灵，并不完全相信，还要演戏求证，这就是科学思想的萌芽。而杜丽娘梦见书生之后，也去花园求证，结果却发现梦想和现实的统一：

“他倚太湖石，立着咱玉婵娟。
待把俺玉山推倒，便日暖玉生烟。”

哈姆雷特演戏求证，要戏子在叔父和母后面前演出毒死父王的剧。叔父看到自己弑君之罪，不能容忍，这时母子之间有两句对话：

母：哈姆雷特，你把你父亲大大得罪了。
子：母亲，你把我父亲大大得罪了。

哈姆雷特以为叔父在偷听他们谈话，一剑刺去；不料刺死的不是叔父，而是奥菲莉娅的父亲波洛涅斯，这也是一个理性的世故人物，他的名言是：

不向人借钱，也并不借钱给谁，
借出去往往就丢了钱也丢了朋友。

不料他这样世故的人物却因为王子的怀疑而丢了性命，这也是情理的矛盾。而在《牡丹亭》中，杜丽娘却是为了爱情而断送了青春，但她命中注定要和柳梦梅成亲，所以一波三折，梦中、死后、复生三度缔结良缘。而莎剧中的一波三折却是父王之死、波洛涅斯之死、最后叔侄母子同归于尽。所以无论以剧情或人物性格而论，《牡丹亭》都比较单纯，莎剧却更加复杂。如以文字而论，莎剧比较巧妙，语意双关；《牡丹亭》却更含蓄深刻，如“把俺玉山推倒，便日暖玉生烟”，说的是“玉山”，指的是丽娘的玉体；说的是“生烟”，指的是男女的欢情，犹如《西厢记》中的“露滴牡丹开”一样，同时这也说明李商隐《锦瑟》中的“蓝田日暖玉生烟”隐指的是男欢女爱。由此可见中西文字的不同，英文更重精确，中文更重精炼。这样看来，从其相同处而言，《牡丹亭》和《哈姆雷特》似乎是不可比的；但从其不同处而言，两部名剧又不是不可相提并论的了。

许渊冲

2009年1月20日

第一本

第一出　标　目[1]

【蝶恋花】（末上[2]）忙处抛人闲处住[3]。百计思量，没个为欢处。白日消磨肠断句，世间只有情难诉。玉茗堂前朝复暮[4]，红烛迎人[5]，俊得江山助[6]。但是相思莫相负[7]，牡丹亭上三生路[8]。【汉宫春】杜宝黄堂[9]，生丽娘小姐，爱踏春阳[10]。感梦书生折柳，竟为情伤。写真留记[11]，葬梅花道院凄凉。三年上，有梦梅柳子，于此赴高唐[12]。　果尔回生定配。赴临安取试，寇起淮扬。正把杜公围困，小姐惊惶。教柳郎行探，反遭疑激恼平章[13]。风流况[14]，施行正苦[15]，报中状元郎。

杜丽娘梦写丹青记[16]。
陈教授说下梨花枪。
柳秀才偷载回生女。
杜平章刁打状元郎[17]。

注释

[1]标目：传奇的第一出，也叫“家门引子”，照例说明：一、戏曲的创作缘起（如本出的《蝶恋花》）；二、剧情梗概（如本出的《汉宫春》）。

[2]末：中国古代戏曲脚色，扮演年纪较大的男人。

[3]忙处抛人闲处住：忙处抛人，指离开繁乱的官场。闲处，指闲散的地方，这里是指作者汤显祖的家乡临川。

[4]玉茗堂：汤显祖住所的名称，以玉茗（白山茶）花而得名。

[5]红烛迎人：《全唐诗》卷九韩翃《赠李翼》："楼前红烛夜迎人。"

[6]俊得江山助：江山之美使文章为之生色。

[7]但是：只要。

[8]牡丹亭上三生路：牡丹亭是本剧男女主人公约定再世姻缘的地方。

[9]黄堂：本指太守的厅堂，代指太守。

[10]踏春阳：踏青。

[11]写真：画像。

[12]赴高唐：用楚怀王游高唐梦与神女欢会典故，见宋玉《高唐赋》序。这个故事中提到的高唐、云雨、巫山、阳台、楚台后来都被用来指男女欢会。

[13]平章：官衔，平章军国重事或同平章军国事的省称，宋制相当于丞相。这里指杜宝。

[14]风流况：风流事。

[15]施行：即用刑。行，一本作"刑"。

[16]丹青：原指绘画所用颜色，多用来代称画和绘画。

[17]这四句在形式上是下场诗，内容则是全剧的剧情大要。

第二出 言 怀

【真珠帘】（生上[1]）河东旧族[2]、柳氏名门最。论星宿，连张带鬼。几叶到寒儒[3]，受雨打风吹。谩说书中能富贵[4]，颜如玉，和黄金那里。贫薄把人灰，且养就这浩然之气[5]。【鹧鸪天】[6]“刮尽鲸鳌背上霜[7]，寒儒偏喜住炎方[8]。凭依造化[9]三分福，绍接诗书一脉香。能凿壁[10]，会悬梁[11]，偷天妙手绣文章[12]。必须砍得蟾宫桂[13]，始信人间玉斧长。”小生姓柳，名梦梅，表字春卿。原系唐朝柳州司马柳宗元之后[14]，留家岭南。父亲朝散之职[15]，母亲县君之封[16]。（叹介）所恨俺自小孤单，生事微渺[17]。喜的是今日成人长大，二十过头，志慧聪明，三场得手[18]。只恨未遭时势[19]，不免饥寒。赖有始祖柳州公，带下郭橐驼，柳州衙舍，栽接花果。橐驼遗下一个驼孙，也跟随俺广州种树，相依过活。虽然如此，不是男儿结果之场。每日情思昏昏，忽然半月之前，做下一梦。梦到一园，梅花树下，立着个美人，不长不短，如送如迎。说道：“柳生，柳生，遇俺方有姻缘之分，发迹之期[20]。”因此改名梦梅，春卿为字。正是：“梦短梦长俱是梦，年来年去是何年！”

【九回肠】【解三酲】虽则俺改名换字，俏魂儿未卜先知[21]？定佳期盼煞蟾宫桂，柳梦梅不卖查梨。还则怕嫦娥妒色花颓气，等的俺梅子酸心柳皱眉，浑如醉。【三学士】无萤凿遍了邻家壁[22]，甚东墙不许人窥[23]！有一日春光暗度黄金柳，雪意冲开了白玉梅。【急三枪】那时节走马在章台内[24]，丝儿翠、笼定个百花魁[25]。虽然这般说，有个朋友韩子才，是韩昌黎之后[26]，寄居赵佗王台[27]。他虽是香火秀才[28]，却有些谈吐，不免随喜一会[29]。

门前梅柳烂春晖，张窈窕
梦见君王觉后疑。王昌龄
心似百花开未得，曹　松
托身须上万年枝。韩　偓[30]

注释

[1]生：传奇中的男主角，相当于元杂剧中的正末。传奇中的男角除生外，还有末、外、净、丑等。

[2]河东旧族：柳姓是河东郡的望族、大姓。

[3]几叶：几代。

[4]谩说：枉说，说什么。

[5]浩然之气：刚直博大之气，指儒者的修养。

[6]以下是生角的上场诗。上场诗可以引用前人现成的诗词，也可以由剧作家自撰。剧作家引用前人的句子时，常加以改动。

[7]刮尽鲸鳌背上霜：喻指刻苦力学，处境却没有改善，贫寒更甚。

[8]炎方：南方。

[9]造化：造物主，上天。

[10]凿壁：汉代匡衡好学，家贫，晚上点不起灯，就在墙壁上凿一个孔，借孔隙里射进的邻居的灯光读书。

[11]悬梁：汉代孙敬读书时怕睡着，就用绳子将头髻挂在梁上，一打瞌睡，就会被拉醒。

[12]偷天妙手：言文才之高。

[13]砍得蟾宫桂：折取月宫的桂枝，古代用作登第的代称。蟾宫，月宫，相传月中有蟾蜍。

[14]唐朝柳州司马柳宗元：唐代文学家柳宗元，曾任永州司马、柳州刺史。司马，州郡的属官。

[15]朝散：朝散大夫，散职文官。

[16]县君：唐制，五品官的妻子封县君。

[17]生事微渺：指生活困难。生事，谋生之事，生活。

[18]三场得手：指取得举人资格。科举时代，童生经考试及格，成为生员（秀才），再通过乡试，成为举人。举人还要参加会试、廷试，通过者为进士。乡、会试都分三场，一场考三天。得手，顺利，称心。

[19]未遭时势：没有遇到机会，指还没有做官。

[20]发迹：飞黄腾达，也指做官。

[21]俏魂儿：指梦中的美人。

[22]萤：晋代车胤好学，家贫，买不起灯油，夏天以练囊装很多萤火虫照明读书。

[23]甚东墙不许人窥：从上句“邻家壁”联想到“东墙”，暗用宋玉“东家之子”的典故。

[24]章台：秦汉时代宫殿名，后用来指京城内娱乐场所聚集的繁华之地。

[25]丝儿翠，笼定个百花魁：官宦人家要我接受丝鞭，和他们的小姐结亲。丝儿翠，即翠丝儿，丝鞭，这是为了押韵而倒文；接受女方家的丝鞭，是古人订婚的一种仪式。百花魁，指梦中的美人。

[26]韩昌黎：指唐代文学家韩愈，他自称郡望为昌黎韩氏，世称昌黎先生。

[27]赵佗王台：即越王台，在今广州北面越秀山上，相传为赵佗王所筑。

[28]香火秀才：即奉祀生。因其为贤圣之后，可不经科举考试而赐秀才功名，管理先祖祠庙的祭祀。第二本第一出中说“表请敕封小生为昌黎祠香火秀才”，可证。

[29]随喜：指游览寺院。

[30]本剧每出结尾的下场诗，全部采用唐诗，诗句与原作时有出入。

第三出 训 女

【满庭芳】（外扮杜太守上）西蜀名儒，南安太守[1]，几番廊庙江湖[2]。紫袍金带[3]，功业未全无。华发不堪回首[4]。意抽簪万里桥西[5]，还只怕君恩未许，五马欲踟躕[6]。“一生名宦守南安，莫作寻常太守看。到来只饮官中水[7]，归去惟看屋外山。”自家南安太守杜宝，表字子充，乃唐朝杜子美之后[8]。流落巴蜀，年过五旬。想廿岁登科[9]，三年出守，清名惠政，播在人间。内有夫人甄氏，乃魏朝甄皇后嫡派[10]。此家峨眉山，见世出贤德。夫人单生小女，才貌端妍，唤名丽娘，未议婚配。看起自来淑女，无不知书。今日政有余闲，不免请出夫人，商议此事。正是：“中郎学富单传女[11]，伯道官贫更少儿。”

【绕池游】（老旦上[12]）甄妃洛浦，嫡派来西蜀，封大郡南安杜母[13]。（见介）（外）“老拜名邦无甚德，（老旦）妾沾封诰有何功[14]！（外）春来闺阁闲多少？（老旦）也长向花阴课女工[15]。”（外）女工一事，想女儿精巧过人。看来古今贤淑，多晓诗书。他日嫁一书生，不枉了谈吐相称。你意下如何？（老旦）但凭尊意。

【前腔】[16]（贴持酒台，随旦上）娇莺欲语，眼见春如许。寸草心，怎报的春光一二[17]！（见介）爹娘万福[18]。（外）孩儿，后面捧着酒肴，是何主意？（旦跪介）今日春光明媚，爹娘宽坐后堂，女孩儿敢进三爵之觞[19]，少效千春之祝。（外笑介）生受你[20]。

【玉山颓】（旦进酒介）爹娘万福，女孩儿无限欢娱。坐黄堂百岁春光，进美酒一家天禄[21]。祝萱花椿树[22]，虽则是子生迟暮，守得见这蟠桃熟[23]。（合）且提壶，花间竹下长引着凤凰雏[24]。（外）春香，酌小姐一杯。

【前腔】吾家杜甫，为飘零老愧妻孥。（泪介）夫人，我比子美公公更可怜也。他还有念老夫诗句男儿，俺则有学母氏画眉娇女。（老旦）相公休焦，傥然招得好女婿，与儿子一般。（外笑介）可一般呢！（老旦）“做门楣”古语[25]，为甚的这叨叨絮絮，才到中年路。（合前[26]）（外）女孩儿，把台盏收去。（旦下介）（外）叫春香。俺问你小姐终日绣房，有何生活[27]？（贴）绣房中则是绣。（外）绣的许多？（贴）绣了打绵[28]。（外）甚么绵？（贴）睡眠。（外）好哩，好哩。夫人，你才说“长向花阴课女工”，却纵容女孩儿闲眠，是何家教？叫女孩儿。（旦上）爹爹有何分付？（外）适问春香，你白日眠睡，是何道理？假如刺绣余闲，有架上图书，可以寓目。他日到人家，知书知礼，父母光辉。这都是你娘亲失教也。

【玉抱肚】宦囊清苦，也不曾诗书误儒。你好些时做客为儿[29]，有一日把家当户。是为爹的疏散不儿拘，道的个为娘是女模[30]。

【前腔】（老旦）眼前儿女，俺为娘心苏体劬[31]。娇养他掌上明珠，出落的人中美玉[32]。儿呵，爹三分说话你自心模，难道八字梳头做目呼[33]。

【前腔】（旦）黄堂父母，倚娇痴惯习如愚。刚打的秋千画图[34]，闲榻着鸳鸯绣谱[35]。从今后茶余饭饱破工夫，玉镜台前插架书。（老旦）虽然如此，要个女先生讲解才好。（外）不能勾。

【前腔】后堂公所[36]，请先生则是黉门腐儒[37]。（老旦）女儿呵，怎念遍的孔子诗书，但略识周公礼数[38]。（合）不枉了银娘玉姐只做个纺砖儿，谢女班姬女校书。（外）请先生不难，则要好生管待。

【尾声】说与你夫人爱女休禽犊[39]，馆明师茶饭须清楚[40]。你看俺治国齐家、也则是数卷书。

往年何事乞西宾[41]，柳宗元
主领春风只在君[42]。王　建
伯道暮年无嗣子，苗　发
女中谁是卫夫人[43]？刘禹锡

注释

[1]南安：宋代有南安军。明代设府，属江西省。

[2]几番廊庙江湖：几次出仕又退隐。廊庙，指在朝廷做官；江湖，指在野，不做官。

[3]紫袍金带：贵官的服装。

[4]华发：头发花白，指年事已高。

[5]意抽簪万里桥西：想到故乡去归隐。做官的人用簪子束发戴冠，抽簪即不束发戴冠，引申为归隐之意。

[6]五马欲踟蹰：去留不定。五马，古代太守出行，以五匹马驾车。

[7]到来只饮官中水：形容做官廉洁。

[8]杜子美：唐代诗人杜甫，字子美。

[9]登科：唐代设科取士，有明经、进士、明法、明算等科。后来考取进士也称登科。

[10]甄皇后：魏文帝曹丕的皇后甄氏。

[11]中郎学富单传女：中郎，指蔡邕，东汉末著名学者。他只有一个女儿蔡琰，字文姬，是有名的才女。

[12]老旦：戏曲角色，扮演老妇人。

[13]封大郡南安杜母：杜宝妻封为南安郡夫人。郡夫人，宋代命妇（受朝廷封号的女性）的一个等级。

[14]封诰：五品以上命妇所受的诰命（封号）。

[15]女工：即女红，指纺织、刺绣、缝纫等工作，古代认为是女性必须具备的技能。

[16]前腔：南曲中指某一曲牌和前面相同。

[17]寸草心，怎报的春光一二：比喻父母恩情很深，报答不了，犹如小草报答不了春光的化育之恩。语出唐孟郊诗《游子吟》："谁言寸草心，报得三春晖。"

[18]万福：古代妇女的一种礼节，敛衽屈身向人行礼，并道万福。

[19]三爵之觞：进三杯酒。爵、觞，都是酒器。

[20]生受：辛苦，麻烦，这里是有劳、道谢的意思。

[21]天禄：指酒，《汉书•食货志》："酒者天之美禄。"

[22]萱花椿树：萱花指母，椿树指父。

[23]蟠桃：神话中的仙桃，相传三千年结一次子。这里比喻迟生的儿子。

[24]凤凰雏：喻男孩和女孩。

[25]"做门楣"古语：做门楣，意指女儿嫁得佳婿，可以提高娘家的社会地位。

[26]合前：重复前一曲的末数句。南曲同一曲牌连用两次以上，结尾相同的数句，叫合头，简称合。

[27]生活：指劳动、工作。

[28]打绵：纺棉纱，这里用作"打眠"的谐音。

[29]做客为儿：女儿在母家就像做客一样。

[30]女模：女儿的榜样。

[31]心苏体劬：身体很累，心里却高兴。苏，精神恢复。

[32]出落的：这是长成的意思。

[33]模：即摸；八字梳头，女性的一种发式；目呼，把四字认成目字，指人不识字。全句的意思是，父亲含蓄的话你自己去体会，你一个小姐，不要变成不识字的人。

[34]打：画，动词。

[35]榻：当作搨（拓），拓写字帖。这里指摹画绣谱上的图样。

[36]后堂公所：衙门里面的官员住宅。

[37]黉门：学校。

[38]周公礼数：礼数，礼节。相传周公作《周礼》。

[39]休禽犊：不要溺爱，像鸟兽爱小鸟小兽那样。

[40]明师：有学问的先生。

[41]西宾：也叫西席，代指塾师。古人请老师坐坐西朝东那个座位，以示尊敬。

[42]春风：比喻教育。

[43]卫夫人：卫铄，晋人李矩的妻子，以书法著名。这里泛指有才学的女性。

第四出 腐 叹

【双劝酒】（末扮老儒上）灯窗苦吟，寒酸撒吞[1]。科场苦禁[2]，蹉跎直恁[3]！可怜辜负看书心。吼儿病年来迸侵[4]。“咳嗽病多疏酒盏，村童俸薄减厨烟。争知天上无人住[5]，吊下春愁鹤发仙[6]。”自家南安府儒学生员陈最良[7]，表字伯粹。祖父行医。小子自幼习儒。十二岁进学，超增补廪[8]。观场一十五次[9]。不幸前任宗师[10]，考居劣等停廪。兼且两年失馆，衣食单薄。这些后生都顺口叫我“陈绝粮[11]”。因我医、卜、地理[12]，所事皆知[13]，又改我表字伯粹做“百杂碎”。明年是第六个旬头，也不想甚的了。有个祖父药店，依然开张在此。“儒变医，菜变齑[14]”，这都不在话下。昨日听见本府杜太守，有个小姐，要请先生。好些奔竞的钻去。他可为甚的？乡邦好说话，一也；通关节[15]，二也；撞太岁[16]，三也；穿他门子管家[17]，改窜文卷，四也；别处吹嘘进身，五也；下头官儿怕他，六也；家里骗人，七也。为此七事，没了头要去[18]。他们都不知官衙可是好踏的！况且女学生一发难教[19]，轻不得，重不得。傥然间体面有些不臻[20]，啼不得，笑不得。似我老人家罢了。“正是有书遮老眼，不妨无药散闲愁。”（丑扮府学门子上）“天下秀才穷到底，学中门子老成精。”（见介）陈斋长报喜[21]。（末）何喜？（丑）杜太爷要请个先生教小姐，掌教老爷开了十数名去都不中[22]，说要老成的。我去掌教老爷处禀上了你，太爷有请帖在此。（末）“人之患在好为人师”[23]。（丑）人之饭，有得你吃哩。（末）这等便行。

（行介）

【洞仙歌】（末）咱头巾破了修，靴头绽了兜[24]。（丑）你坐老斋头，衫襟没了后头。（合）砚水漱净口，去承官饭溲，剔牙杖敢黄齑臭。

【前腔】（丑）咱门儿寻事头，你斋长干罢休？（末）要我谢酬，知那里留不留？（合）不论端阳九[25]，但逢出府游，则捻着衫儿袖。（丑）望见府门了。

（丑）世间荣乐本逡巡[26]，李商隐
（末）谁睬髭须白似银？　曹　唐
（丑）风流太守容闲坐，　朱庆余
（合）便有无边求福人。　韩　愈

注 释

[1]撒吞：一作撒哈，装呆，这里有痴心妄想之意。吞，痴呆。

[2]科场苦禁：一直没有考取（举人）。禁，抑止。

[3]直恁：竟然如此。

[4]吼儿病：哮喘病。

[5]争：怎。

[6]鹤发仙：白发仙人，这里指老人，陈最良自喻。

[7]儒学生员：旧时府州县所设立的学堂叫儒学，已进学的儒生就是秀才，也称生员。

[8]超增补廪（lǐn）：生员有定额，额外增加的叫增广生员。补廪，由政府补入名额，供给膳食。

[9]观场：参加考试。

[10]宗师：秀才称主持一省举业的学政为宗师。

[11]陈绝粮：有一次孔子“在陈绝粮”，见《论语•卫灵公》。这个绰号是拿陈最良开玩笑，嘲其贫寒。

[12]地理：堪舆，风水。

[13]所事：凡事。

[14]齑（jī）：咸菜。菜变齑，比喻境况越来越坏。

[15]通关节：受人贿赂，替其在官府里面活动。

[16]撞太岁：依托官府赚人财物。

[17]穿他门子管家：穿，串通。门子，州县长宫的贴身仆役。管家，奴仆中为头管事的。

[18]没了头：拚命。

[19]一发：这里是更加、愈加之意。

[20]不臻：不周到，不完备。

[21]斋长：明代国子监的班长，也泛用作对秀才的敬称。

[22]掌教老爷：即教授，府学的教官。

[23]人之患在好(hào)为人师：语出《孟子•离娄上》。

[24]绽(zhàn)了兜：破了补起来。

[25]端阳九：端阳（阴历五月初五日）和重阳（九月初九）两个节日。

[26]逡巡：这里是来去不定之意。

第五出 延 师

【浣沙溪】（外引贴扮门子，丑扮皂隶上）山色好，讼庭稀。朝看飞鸟暮飞回。印床花落帘垂地[1]。“杜母高风不要攀[2]，甘棠游憩在南安[3]。虽然为政多阴德，尚少阶前玉树兰[4]。”我杜宝出守此间，只有夫人一女。寻个老儒教训他。昨日府学开送一名廪生陈最良。年可六旬，从来饱学。一来可以教授小女，二来可以陪伴老夫。今日放了衙参[5]，分付安排礼酒，叫门子伺候。（众应介）

【前腔】（末儒巾蓝衫上[6]）须抖擞，要拳奇。衣冠欠整老而衰。养浩然分庭还抗礼[7]。（丑禀介）陈斋长到门。（外）就请衙内相见。（丑唱门介[8]）南安府学生员进。（下）（末跪，起揖，又跪介）生员陈最良禀拜。（拜介）（末）“讲学开书院，（外）崇儒引席珍[9]。（末）献酬樽俎列[10]，（外）宾主位班陈[11]。”叫左右，陈斋长在此清叙，着门役散回，家丁伺候。（众应下）（净扮家童上）（外）久闻先生饱学。敢问尊年有几，祖上可也习儒？（末）容禀。

【锁南枝】将耳顺[12]，望古稀，儒冠误人霜鬓丝。（外）近来？（末）君子要知医，悬壶旧家世[13]。（外）原来世医。还有他长？（末）凡杂作，可试为；但诸家，略通的。（外）这等一发有用。

【前腔】闻名久，识面初，果然大邦生大儒。（末）不敢。（外）有女颇知书，先生长训诂[14]。（末）当得[15]。则怕做不得小姐之师。（外）那女学士，你做的班大姑[16]。今日选良辰，叫他拜师傅。（外）院子，敲云板[17]，请小姐出来。

【前腔】（旦引贴上）添眉翠[18]，摇佩珠，绣屏中生成士女图[19]。莲步鲤庭趋[20]，儒门旧家数[21]。（贴）先生来了怎好？（旦）那少不得去。丫头，那贤达女，都是些古镜模[22]。你便略知书，也做好奴仆。（净报介）小姐到。（见介）（外）我儿过来。“玉不琢，不成器；人不学，不知道。[23]”今日吉辰，来拜了先生。（内鼓吹介）（旦拜）学生自愧蒲柳之姿[24]，敢烦桃李之教。（末）愚老恭承捧珠之爱[25]，谬加琢玉之功。（外）春香丫头，向陈师父叩头。着他伴读。（贴叩头介）（末）敢问小姐所读何书？（外）男、女《四书》[26]，他都成诵了。则看些经旨罢。《易经》以道阴阳，义理深奥；《书》以道政事[27]，与妇女没相干；《春秋》、《礼记》，又是孤经[28]；则《诗经》开首便是后妃之德[29]，四个字儿顺口，且是学生家传[30]，习《诗》罢。其余书史尽有，则可惜他是个女儿。

【前腔】我年将半[31]，性喜书，牙签插架三万余[32]。（叹介）我伯道恐无儿，中郎有谁付？先生，他要看的书尽看。有不臻的所在，打丫头。（贴）哎哟！（外）冠儿下[33]，他做个女秘书。小梅香[34]，要防护。（末）谨领。（外）春香伴小姐进衙，我陪先生酒去。（旦拜介）“酒是先生馔[35]，女为君子儒。[36]”（下）（外）请先生后花园饮酒。

（外）门馆无私白日闲[37]，薛　能
（末）百年粗粝腐儒餐。　杜　甫
（外）左家弄玉惟娇女[38]，柳宗元
（合）花里寻师到杏坛[39]。钱　起

注 释

[1]印床：放印章用的文具，形状像床。

[2]杜母：指东汉人杜诗，召信臣和他前后做南阳太守，很受人民爱戴，民谚将他们比为父母。

[3]甘棠：周代召公出巡，曾在甘棠树下休息。后来人民怀念他，作了一首《甘棠》诗，见于《诗经》。后来用甘棠代指好官；这里是杜宝自比。

[4]玉树兰：玉树、芝兰，比喻优秀的子弟。

[5]放了衙参：不办公。衙参，召集官员办事。

[6]蓝衫：明代生员的制服。

[7]分庭还抗礼：指平等相待。

[8]唱门：报出准备进见的客人。

[9]席珍：语出《礼记•儒行》，比喻儒者珍视自己，等待政府的聘用。这里指优秀的儒生。

[10]樽俎：樽，酒器。俎，食器。

[11]位班陈：座位按次序排列好。

[12]耳顺：六十岁。

[13]悬壶：指行医。

[14]训诂：本来指解释字义的专门学问。这里指教人读书。

[15]当得：理当如此。

[16]班大姑：即汉代班昭，曾为宫廷后妃的教师，被称为大家(gū)。

[17]云板：雕绘着云彩的木板或金属片做的打击乐器，寺院、官署中作信号用。

[18]翠：这里指黛，画眉用的深青色颜料。

[19]士女图：美人图，这里指美人。

[20]鲤庭趋：《论语•季氏》说，孔子站在那里，其子孔鲤“趋而过庭”。趋，小跑着过去，表示尊敬。

[21]家数：家法，家风。

[22]镜模：榜样，借鉴。

[23]玉不琢，不成器；人不学，不知道：语出《礼记•学记》。

[24]蒲柳之姿：原意是像蒲柳一样早衰，这里用作自谦。

[25]捧珠之爱：俗称女儿为掌中珠，表示爱惜。

[26]男、女《四书》：男四书，即《大学》《中庸》与《论语》《孟子》，南宋理学家朱熹所编。女四书，封建时代针对女性教育而编写的几种读物。

[27]《书》以道政事：语出《庄子•天下》："《诗》以道志，《书》以道事，《礼》以道行，《乐》以道和，《易》以道阴阳，《春秋》以道名分。"

[28]孤经：这是从"孤"字着眼的打诨之词。

[29]后妃之德：《诗经》第一篇《关雎》，前人将其解说为歌颂后妃之德的作品。

[30]学生家传：杜宝自命为杜甫的后代。学生，对自己的谦称。

[31]半：半百的省词，即五十岁。

[32]牙签插架三万余：形容藏书很多。牙签，古代夹在书上的标签。

[33]冠儿：古礼，男子"二十而冠"，表示成人。

[34]梅香：对丫头的通称。

[35]酒是先生馔：酒是先生吃的。《论语•为政》："有酒食，先生馔。"先生，原文指父兄。

[36]女为君子儒：女儿要学做有德行的读书人。

[37]门馆：这里指家塾。

[38]左家弄玉惟娇女：没有儿子，只得把女儿当作男孩。弄玉，即弄璋，指生男孩子。

[39]杏坛：孔丘讲学之处，在山东曲阜。这里是指教师所在的地方。

第二本

第一出 怅眺

【番卜算】（丑扮韩秀才上）家世大唐年，寄籍潮阳县。越王台上海连天，可是鹏程便[1]？“榕树梢头访古台，下看甲子海门开[2]。越王歌舞今何在？时有鹧鸪飞去来[3]。”自家韩子才。俺公公唐朝韩退之，为上了《破佛骨表》[4]，贬落潮州。一出门蓝关雪阻，马不能前。先祖心里暗暗道，第一程采头罢了[5]。正苦中间，忽然有个湘子侄儿，乃下八洞神仙[6]，蓝缕相见。俺退之公公一发心里不快。呵融冻笔，题一首诗在蓝关草驿之上。末二句单指着湘子说道：“知汝远来应有意，好收吾骨瘴江边。”湘子袖了这诗[7]，长笑一声，腾空而去。果然后来退之公公潮州瘴死[8]，举目无亲。那湘子恰在云端看见，想起前诗，按下云头，收其骨殖[9]。到得衙中，四顾无人，单单则有湘子原妻一个在衙。四目相视，把湘子一点凡心顿起。当时生下一支，留在水潮[10]，传了宗祀。小生乃其嫡派苗裔也。因乱流来广城[11]。官府念是先贤之后，表请敕封小生为昌黎祠香火秀才。寄居赵佗王台子之上。正是：“虽然乞相寒儒[12]，却是仙风道风。”呀，早一位朋友上来。谁也？

【前腔】（生上）经史腹便便[13]，昼梦人还倦。欲寻高耸看云烟，海色光平面。（相见介）（丑）是柳春卿，甚风儿吹的老兄来？（生）偶尔孤游上此台。（丑）这台上风光尽可矣。（生）则无奈登临不快哉。（丑）小弟此间受用也。（生）小弟想起来，到是不读书的人受用。（丑）谁？（生）赵佗王[14]便是。

【锁寒窗】祖龙飞、鹿走中原[15]，尉佗啊，他倚定着摩崖半壁天[16]。称孤道寡[17]，是他英雄本然。白占了江山，猛起些宫殿。似吾侪读尽万卷书，可有半块土么？那半部上山河不见[18]。（合）由天，那攀今吊古也徒然，荒台古树寒烟。（丑）小弟看兄气象言谈，似有无聊之叹。先祖昌黎公有云："不患有司之不明，只患文章之不精；不患有司之不公，只患经书之不通。"老兄，还则怕工夫有不到处。（生）这话休提。比如我公公柳宗元，与你公公韩退之，他都是饱学才子，却也时运不济。你公公错题了《佛骨表》，贬职潮阳。我公公则为在朝阳殿与王叔文丞相下棋子，惊了圣驾，直贬做柳州司马。都是边海烟瘴地方。那时两公一路而来，旅舍之中，两个挑灯细论。你公公说道："宗元，宗元，我和你两人文章，三六九比势[19]：我有《王泥水传》，你便有《梓人传》；我有《毛中书传》，你便有《郭驼子传》；我有《祭鳄鱼文》，你便有《捕蛇者说》。这也罢了。则我《进平淮西碑》，取奉取奉[20]朝廷，你却又进个平淮西的雅。一篇一篇，你都放俺不过。恰如今贬窜烟方[21]，也合着一处。岂非时乎，运乎，命乎！"韩兄，这长远的事休提了。假如俺和你论如常，难道便应这等寒落。因何俺公公造下一篇《乞巧文》，到俺二十八代元孙，再不曾乞得一些巧来？便是你公公立意做下《送穷文》，到老兄二十几辈了，还不曾送的个穷去？算来都则为时运二字所亏。（丑）是也。春卿兄，

【前腔】你费家资制买书田[22]，怎知他卖向明时不值钱[23]。虽然如此，你看赵佗王当时，也是个秀才陆贾[24]，拜为奉使中大夫到此。赵佗王多少尊重他。他归朝燕，黄金累千。那时汉高皇厌见读书之人，但有个带儒巾的[25]，都拿来溺尿。这陆贾秀才，端然带了四方巾，深衣大摆[26]，去见汉高皇。那高皇望

见，这又是个掉尿鳖子的来了[27]。便迎着陆贾骂道："你老子用马上得天下，何用诗书？"那陆生有趣，不多应他，只回他一句："陛下马上取天下，能以马上治之乎？"汉高皇听了，哑然一笑，说道："便依你说。不管什么文字，念了与寡人听之。"陆大夫不慌不忙，袖里出一卷文字，恰是平日灯窗下纂集的《新语》一十三篇，高声奏上。那高皇才听了一篇，龙颜大喜。后来一篇一篇，都喝采称善。立封他做个关内侯。那一日好不气象[28]！休道汉高皇，便是那两班文武，见者皆呼万岁。一言掷地，万岁喧天。（生叹介）则俺连篇累牍无人见。（合前）（丑）再问春卿，在家何以为生？（生）寄食园公[29]。（丑）依小弟说，不如干谒些须[30]，可图前进。（生）你不知，今人少趣哩。（丑）老兄可知？有个钦差识宝中郎苗老先生，到是个知趣人。今秋任满，例于香山嶴多宝寺中赛宝[31]。那时一往何如？（生）领教。

应念愁中恨索居[32]，段成式
青云器业俺全疏[33]。李商隐
越王自指高台笑，　皮日休
刘项原来不读书[34]。章　碣

注释

[1]鹏程：前程远大。典出《庄子•逍遥游》：“鹏之徙于南溟也，水击三千里，抟扶摇而上者九万里。”

[2]甲子海门：广东陆丰东南有甲子门海口，形势险要。

[3]越王歌舞今何在？时有鹧鸪飞去来：语出李白诗《越中览古》：“越王勾践破吴归，义士还家尽锦衣。宫女如花满春殿，只今惟有鹧鸪飞。”这里因南越王赵佗和越王勾践称号相似而借用。

[4]破佛骨表：即《论佛骨表》。元和十四年，唐宪宗迎接释迦佛骨一节入宫，韩愈上表反对，被贬为潮州刺史。

[5]采头罢了：兆头不好的意思。采头，兆头。

[6]下八洞神仙：道家传说有所谓上八洞神仙、下八洞神仙。一般所说八仙即汉钟离、张果老、韩湘子、李铁拐、曹国舅、吕洞宾、蓝采和、何仙姑。

[7]袖：动词，放入衣袖内。

[8]退之公公潮州瘴死：这里说的韩愈事迹是编造出来的，不符合历史事实。

[9]骨殖：骸骨。

[10]水潮：应是潮州附近的地名。

[11]广城：广州。

[12]乞相：寒乞相，穷相。

[13]经史腹便便：满肚子都是学问。

[14]赵佗王：即赵佗。秦末为南海尉，又称尉佗。秦亡，赵佗自立为南越武王。汉高祖派陆贾去封他为南越王。后他自立为南越武帝，汉孝文帝派陆贾再次出使，说服他废去帝号，归顺汉朝。《史记》卷一百十三有传。

[15]祖龙飞、鹿走中原：祖龙，指秦始皇；飞，死。鹿走中原，比喻政权动荡不定。

[16]倚定着摩崖半壁天：倚定着摩崖，凭着天险；半壁天，割据一方。

[17]称孤道寡：自立为王。王、小国君主自称孤，皇帝自称寡人。

[18]半部：指半部《论语》。相传宋代赵普曾经对宋太宗说，他以半部《论语》帮助太祖（赵匡胤）打天下，以另外半部帮助太宗治理国家。

[19]三六九比势：谓旗鼓相当，势均力敌。

[20]取奉：取奉，原指向皇帝效劳、贡献，这里是趋奉的谐音，奉承、讨好的意思。

[21]烟方：瘴气流行的地区。

[22]制买书田：旧时认为买书和买田一样，因买田可以收租，读书可以升官发财，都有利可图。

[23]明时：政治清明的时代。

[24]陆贾：汉初政治家、辩士，曾受汉高祖和汉文帝之命，往海南招谕赵佗。

[25]儒巾：古代读书人戴的头巾。

[26]深衣：古人所穿形似长袍的衣服。

[27]尿鳖子：尿壶。

[28]气象：这里作形容词用，犹言神气。

[29]园公：园丁。

[30]干谒：向有地位的人求请。

[31]香山嶼：在今广东中山境内，古时是对外贸易港，明代为洋商聚居处。

[32]索居：独居。

[33]青云器业：做官的才能。青云，爬得很高，指做大官。

[34]刘、项：指汉高祖刘邦和楚霸王项羽。

第二出 闺塾

（末上）“吟余改抹前春句，饭后寻思午晌茶。蚁上案头沿砚水，蜂穿窗眼咂瓶花。”我陈最良杜衙设帐[1]，杜小姐家传《毛诗》[2]。极承老夫人管待。今日早膳已过，我且把毛注潜玩一遍。（念介）“关关雎鸠，在河之洲。窈窕淑女，君子好逑[3]。”好者好也，逑者求也。（看介）这早晚了[4]，还不见女学生进馆。却也娇养的凶。待我敲三声云板。（敲云板介）春香，请小姐解书。

【绕池游】（旦引贴捧书上）素妆才罢，缓步书堂下。对净几明窗潇洒。（贴）《昔氏贤文》[5]，把人禁杀，恁时节[6]则好教鹦哥唤茶[7]。（见介）（旦）先生万福，（贴）先生少怪。（末）凡为女子，鸡初鸣，咸盥、漱、栉、笄，问安于父母[8]。日出之后，各供其事。如今女学生以读书为事，须要早起。（旦）以后不敢了。（贴）知道了。今夜不睡，三更时分，请先生上书。（末）昨日上的《毛诗》，可温习？（旦）温习了。则待讲解。（末）你念来。（旦念书介）“关关雎鸠，在河之洲。窈窕淑女，君子好逑。”（末）听讲。“关关雎鸠”，雎鸠是个鸟，关关鸟声也。（贴）怎样声儿？（末作鸠声）（贴学鸠声诨介）（末）此鸟性喜幽静，在河之洲。（贴）是了。不是昨日是前日，不是今年是去年，俺衙内关着个斑鸠儿，被小姐放去，一去去在何知州家[9]。（末）胡说，这是兴[10]。（贴）兴个甚的那？（末）兴者起也。起那下头窈窕淑女，是幽闲女子，有那等君子好好的来求他。（贴）为甚好好的求他？（末）多嘴哩。（旦）师父，依注解书，学生自会。但把《诗经》大意，敷演一番[11]。

【掉角儿】（末）论《六经》，《诗经》最葩[12]，闺门内许多风雅：有指证，姜嫄产哇[13]；不嫉妒，后妃贤达[14]。更有那咏鸡鸣，伤燕羽，泣江皋，思汉广，洗净铅华[15]。有风有化[16]，宜室宜家[17]。（旦）这经文偌多？（末）《诗》三百[18]，一言以蔽之，没多些，只“无邪”两字，付与儿家。书讲了。春香取文房四宝来模字[19]。（贴下取上）纸、墨、笔、砚在此。（末）这什么墨？（旦）丫头错拿了，这是螺子黛，画眉的。（末）这什么笔？（旦作笑介）这便是画眉细笔。（末）俺从不曾见。拿去，拿去！这是什么纸？（旦）薛涛笺[20]。（末）拿去，拿去。只拿那蔡伦造的来[21]。这是什么砚？是一个是两个？（旦）鸳鸯砚。（末）许多眼[22]？（旦）泪眼[23]。（末）哭什么子？一发换了来。（贴背介）好个标老儿[24]！待换去。（下换上）这可好？（末看介）着。（旦）学生自会临书。春香还劳把笔。（末）看你临。（旦写字介）（末看惊介）我从不曾见这样好字。这什么格？（旦）是卫夫人传下美女簪花之格[25]。（贴）待俺写个奴婢学夫人[26]。（旦）还早哩。（贴）先生，学生领出恭牌[27]。（下）（旦）敢问师母尊年？（末）目下平头六十[28]。（旦）学生待绣对鞋儿上寿，请个样儿。（末）生受了。依《孟子》上样儿，做个“不知足而为屦”罢了[29]。（旦）还不见春香来。（末）要唤他么？（末叫三度介）（贴上）害淋的。（旦作恼介）劣丫头那里来？（贴笑介）溺尿去来。原来有座大花园。花明柳绿，好耍子哩。（末）哎也，不攻书，花园去。待俺取荆条来。（贴）荆条做什么？

【前腔】女郎行[30]、那里应文科判衙[31]？止不过识字儿书涂嫩鸦[32]。（起介）（末）古人读书，有囊萤的，趁月亮的[33]。（贴）待映月，耀蟾蜍眼花；待囊萤，把虫蚁儿[34]活支煞[35]。（末）悬梁、刺股呢[36]？（贴）比似你悬了梁，损头发；刺了股，添疤痆[37]。有甚光华！（内叫卖花介）（贴）小姐，你听一声声卖花，把读书声差。（末）又引逗小姐哩。待俺当真打一下。（末做打介）（贴闪介[38]）你待打、打这哇哇，桃李门墙[39]，崄把负荆人唬煞[40]。（贴抢荆条投地介）（旦）死丫头，唐突了师父[41]，快跪下。（贴跪介）（旦）师父看他初犯，容学生责认一遭儿。

【前腔】手不许把秋千索拿，脚不许把花园路踏。（贴）则瞧罢。（旦）还嘴，这招风嘴[42]，把香头来绰疤[43]；招花眼，把绣针儿签瞎[44]。（贴）瞎了中甚用？（旦）则要你守砚台，跟书案，伴“诗云”，陪“子曰”，没的争差[45]。（贴）争差些罢。（旦挦贴发介[46]）则问你几丝儿头发，几条背花[47]？敢也怕些些夫人堂上那些家法[48]。（贴）再不敢了。（旦）可知道？（末）也罢，松这一遭儿。起来。（贴起介）

【尾声】（末）女弟子则争个不求闻达[49]，和男学生一般儿教法。你们工课完了，方可回衙。咱和公相陪话去。（合）怎辜负的这一弄明窗新绛纱[50]。（末下）（贴作背后指末骂介）村老牛[51]，痴老狗，一些趣也不知。（旦作扯介）死丫头，“一日为师，终身为父”，他打不的你？俺且问你那花园在那里？（贴做不说）（旦做笑问介）（贴指介）兀那不是[52]！（旦）可有什么景致？（贴）景致么，有亭台六七座，秋千一两架。绕的流觞曲水[53]，面着太湖山石[54]。名花异草，委实华丽。（旦）原来有这等一个所在，且回衙去。

（旦）也曾飞絮谢家庭[55]，李山甫

（贴）欲化西园蝶未成。张　泌
（旦）无限春愁莫相问，赵　嘏
（合）绿阴终借暂时行。张　祜

注释

[1]设帐：教书。

[2]《毛诗》：战国毛亨著《毛诗故训传》，解释《诗经》，简称《毛诗》。

[3]“关关雎鸠”四句：《诗经》第一首诗《关雎》的头四句。

[4]早晚：时候。

[5]《昔氏贤文》：书名，用格言编成的一种初学读本。下文的“禁杀”，意思是拘束死了。

[6]恁时节：这时候。

[7]鹦哥：鹦鹉。

[8]鸡初鸣，咸盥、漱、栉、笄，问安于父母：见于《礼记•内则》，为旧时代对子女的要求。

[9]知州：州的行政长官。何知州与“河之洲”谐音。

[10]兴：风、雅、颂、赋、比、兴称为《诗》的六义。风、雅、颂指《诗》的不同体制；赋、比、兴指《诗》的作法。兴，即物起兴，民歌开头常用这种手法。

[11]敷演：这里是解释的意思。

[12]论《六经》，《诗经》最葩：《六经》中以《诗经》最有文采。《六经》，《易》《诗》《书》《礼》《乐》《春秋》六部儒家经典著作的合称。

[13]姜嫄产哇：古代传说，姜嫄是黄帝的曾孙帝喾的妃子，她踩了天帝的大脚趾印，因而怀孕，生下后稷。哇，通娃。

[14]不嫉妒，后妃贤达：《诗•周南》中的《樛木》《螽斯》等篇，旧时注解认为都是写后妃不妒忌的。

[15]洗净铅华：归之于朴素。铅华，铅粉，古代女性搽脸用。

[16]有风有化：有教育意义。

[17]宜室宜家：女儿在夫家，使一家和顺。

[18]《诗》三百：《诗经》收录诗歌三百零五篇，三百是整数。

[19]文房四宝：即下文所说纸、墨、笔、砚。

[20]薛涛笺：相传是唐代才女薛涛所制的笺纸。

[21]蔡伦：东汉人，发明了纸。

[22]眼：砚眼，砚石经磨制后现出的天然石纹，圆晕如眼，有不同颜色。

[23]泪眼：广东高要端溪出产的砚叫端砚，它的眼不很清润明朗的叫泪眼，次于活眼，但比死眼好。死眼又比没有的好。

[24]标老儿：犹如说土老儿，不知趣的人。

[25]美女簪花之格：形容书法娟秀。

[26]奴婢学夫人：因气质不同而学不像的意思。

[27]出恭牌：明代试场，考生上厕所要请假，凭牌出入。

[28]平头：平头就是齐头，凡计数逢十，叫齐头数。

[29]不知足而为屦：语出《孟子•告子上》，这里用来嘲讽陈最良的书呆子气。屦，鞋子。

[30]行：用在人称词之后，有“辈”、“家”的意思。

[31]应文科判衙：去应考，考取后做官坐堂办事。

[32]书涂嫩鸦：随便写几个字儿。

[33]趁月亮的：南齐江泌家贫，点不起灯，晚上在月亮下读书。

[34]虫蚁儿：泛指昆虫，这里指萤火虫。

[35]活支煞：活活地弄死。

[36]刺股：战国时苏秦刻苦学习，用锥子刺大腿防止自己睡着。

[37]疤(niè)：疤。

[38]闪：躲避。

[39]门墙：指师门。《论语•子张》："夫子之墙数仞，不得其门而入。"

[40]负荆人：身背荆条向人请罪的人，这里指有过错的人。

[41]唐突：冒犯。

[42]招风：招惹是非。

[43]把香头来绰疤：用点着的香来戳，烧一个疤。绰，戳。

[44]签：刺。

[45]没的争差：这里是不要出差错的意思。

[46]挦（xún）：用手指扯、拔。

[47]背花：背上被鞭打的伤痕。

[48]家法：旧时家长责打家人的鞭子等用具。

[49]女弟子则争个不求闻达：女学生不要做官，这一点（和男的）不一样。

[50]一弄：一派、一带。

[51]村：粗野。

[52]兀那：兀那，兀谁，意思是那、谁，但语气较强。兀，兀的，犹言这。

[53]流觞曲水：宜于游宴的曲水。流觞，古代人在修禊日把装酒的杯子（觞）放在水上，顺水流下去。

[54]太湖山石：太湖石堆叠的假山。

[55]也曾飞絮谢家庭：意思是说自己像谢道韫一样有诗才。

第三出 肃 苑[1]

【一江风】（贴上）小春香，一种在人奴上[2]，画阁里从娇养。侍娘行，弄粉调朱，贴翠拈花，惯向妆台傍。陪他理绣床，陪他烧夜香。小苗条吃的是夫人杖。“花面丫头十三四[3]，春来绰约省人事。终须等着个助情花[4]，处处相随步步觑。”俺春香日夜跟随小姐。看他名为国色，实守家声。嫩脸娇羞，老成尊重。只因老爷延师教授，读到《毛诗》第一章：“窈窕淑女，君子好逑。”悄然废书而叹曰：“圣人之情，尽见于此矣。今古同怀，岂不然乎？”春香因而进言：“小姐读书困闷，怎生消遣则个[5]？”小姐一会沉吟[6]，逡巡而起。便问道：“春香，你教我怎生消遣那[7]？”俺便应道：“小姐，也没个甚法儿，后花园走走罢。”小姐说：“死丫头，老爷闻知怎好？”春香应说：“老爷下乡，有几日了。”小姐低回不语者久之[8]，方才取过历书选看。说明日不佳，后日欠好，除大后日，是个小游神吉期[9]。预唤花郎，扫清花径。我一时应了，则怕老夫人知道。却也由他。且自叫那小花郎分付去。呀，回廊那厢，陈师父来了。正是：“年光到处皆堪赏[10]，说与痴翁总不知。”

【前腔】（末上）老书堂，暂借扶风帐[11]。日暖钩帘荡。呀，那回廊，小立双鬟[12]，似语无言，近看如何相[13]？是春香，问你恩官在那厢？夫人在那厢？女书生怎不把书来上？（贴）原来是陈师父。俺小姐这几日没工夫上书。（末）为甚？（贴）听呵，

【前腔】甚年光！忒煞通明相[14]，所事关情况。（末）有什么情况？（贴）老师父还不知，老爷怪你哩。（末）何事？（贴）说你讲《毛诗》，毛的忒精了[15]。小姐呵，为诗章，讲动情肠。（末）则讲了个“关关雎鸠”。（贴）故此了。小姐说，关了的雎鸠，尚然有洲渚之兴，可以人而不如鸟乎！书要埋头，那景致则抬头望。如今吩咐，明后日游后花园。（末）为甚去游？（贴）他平白地为春伤。因春去的忙，后花园要把春愁漾[16]。（末）一发不该了。

【前腔】论娘行，出入人观望，步起须屏障[17]。春香，你师父靠天也六十来岁，从不晓得伤个春，从不曾游个花园。（贴）为甚？（末）你不知。孟夫子说的好，圣人千言万语，则要人“收其放心”[18]。但如常，看甚春伤？要甚春游？你放春归，怎把心儿放？小姐既不上书，我且告归几日。春香啊，你寻常到讲堂[19]，时常向琐窗[20]，怕燕泥香点涴在琴书上。我去了。“绣户女郎闲斗草[21]，下帷老子不窥园[22]。”（下）（贴吊场[23]）且喜陈师父去了。叫花郎在么？（叫介）花郎！

【普贤歌】（丑扮小花郎醉上）一生花里小随衙[24]，偷去街头学卖花。令史们将我揸[25]，祗候们将我搭，狠烧刀[26]、险把我嫩盘肠生灌杀。（见介）春姐在此。（贴）好打。私出衙前骗酒，这几日菜也不送。（丑）有菜夫。（贴）水也不枧[27]。（丑）有水夫。（贴）花也不送。（丑）每早送花，夫人一分，小姐一分。（贴）还有一分哩？（丑）这该打。（贴）你叫什么名字？（丑）花郎。（贴）你把花郎的意思，挡个曲儿俺听。挡的好，饶打。（丑）使得。

【梨花儿】小花郎看尽了花成浪，则春姐花沁的水洸浪。和你这日高头偷眼眼，嗏，好花枝干鳖了作么朗！（贴）待俺还你也哥。

【前腔】小花郎做尽花儿浪，小郎当夹细的大当郎？（丑）哎哟，（贴）俺待到老爷回时说一浪[28]，（采丑发介）嗦，敢几个小榔头把你分的朗[29]。（丑倒介）罢了，姐姐为甚事光降小园？（贴）小姐大后日来瞧花园，好些扫除花径。（丑）知道了。

东郊风物正薰馨， 崔日用
应喜家山接女星[30]。陈 陶
莫遣儿童触红粉[31]，韦应物
便教莺语太丁宁。 杜 甫

注释

[1]肃苑：打扫园林。肃，整肃，这里指打扫。
[2]一种：同样。
[3]花面：古代女性用花片贴在脸上作为装饰。
[4]助情花：据说是安禄山献给唐明皇的一种春药。
[5]则个：用在句子结尾，表示加强语气。
[6]沉吟：考虑、思忖。
[7]那：这里同哪，语尾词。
[8]低回：徘徊。
[9]小游神：古人出行要选择吉日，避免凶煞。所谓小游神当值的日子，被认为是吉日。
[10]年光：春光。
[11]扶风帐：指教书。

[12]双鬟：古代少女所梳发髻式样。这里指春香。

[13]近看如何相：走近些看看是谁。

[14]忒煞通明相：太聪明的模样儿。

[15]精：原指精深，这里意含讽刺，意谓奇怪。

[16]春愁漾：排遣春愁。

[17]出入人观望，步起须屏障：古代女子出外要把脸孔遮住，不使人看见。

[18]圣人千言万语，则要人“收其放心”：圣人，指孟子，他认为人性本善，做学问就是把丧失了的本性（心）重新找回来。

[19]寻常：平常，这里作常常解。

[20]琐窗：装饰得很好的窗子，这里指书房。

[21]绣户：闺房。

[22]窥园：汉代董仲舒在帷帐内专心治学，三年都不去看一眼园圃。

[23]吊场：一出戏的结尾，其他演员都下场，留一二人念下场诗，叫吊场。这里是一出戏中的转场，由春香的说白转到另一个场面。

[24]随衙：随班，就是跟随，侍候。

[25]揸：抓。

[26]烧刀：烧酒。

[27]枧：水管。这里作动词用，接通水管。

[28]说一浪：犹言说一下、说一番。

[29]敢几个小榔头把你分的朗：犹言怕只要几棒槌就把你打成两段。榔头，棒槌。

[30]女星：女星，二十八宿之一，主扬州。

[31]莫遣儿童触红粉：指不要让小儿女懂男女之间的事。

第四出 惊 梦

【绕池游】（旦上）梦回莺啭，乱煞年光遍[1]。人立小庭深院。（贴）炷尽沉烟[2]，抛残绣线，恁今春关情似去年？【乌夜啼】“（旦）晓来望断梅关[3]，宿妆残[4]。（贴）你侧着宜春髻子恰凭阑[5]。（旦）翦不断，理还乱[6]，闷无端。（贴）已分付催花莺燕借春看。”（旦）春香，可曾叫人扫除花径？（贴）分付了。（旦）取镜台衣服来。（贴取镜台衣服上）“云髻罢梳还对镜，罗衣欲换更添香。”镜台衣服在此。

【步步娇】（旦）袅晴丝吹来闲庭院[7]，摇漾春如线。停半晌、整花钿。没揣[8]菱花[9]，偷人半面，迤逗的彩云偏。（行介）步香闺怎便把全身现！（贴）今日穿插的好。

【醉扶归】（旦）你道翠生生出落的裙衫儿茜，艳晶晶花簪八宝填[10]，可知我常一生儿爱好是天然[11]。恰三春好处无人见[12]。不堤防沉鱼落雁鸟惊喧[13]，则怕的羞花闭月花愁颤。（贴）早茶时了，请行。（行介）你看：“画廊金粉半零星，池馆苍苔一片青。踏草怕泥新绣袜[14]，惜花疼煞小金铃。”（旦）不到园林，怎知春色如许！

【皂罗袍】原来姹紫嫣红开遍[15]，似这般都付与断井颓垣。良辰美景奈何天，赏心乐事谁家院！恁般景致，我老爷和奶奶再不提起。（合）朝飞暮卷，云霞翠轩；雨丝风片，烟波画船——锦屏人忒看的这韶光贱[16]！（贴）是花都放了[17]，那牡丹还早。

【好姐姐】（旦）遍青山啼红了杜鹃[18]，观之不足由他缱[19]，便赏遍了十二亭台是枉然。到不如兴尽回家闲过遣。（作到介）（贴）“开我西阁门，展我东阁床[20]。瓶插映山紫[21]，炉添沉水香。”小姐，你歇息片时，俺瞧老夫人去也。（下）（旦叹介）“默地游春转，小试宜春面[22]。”春呵，得和你两留连，春去如何遣？咳，恁般天气，好困人也。春香那里？（作左右瞧介）（又低首沉吟介）天呵，春色恼人，信有之乎！常观诗词乐府，古之女子，因春感情，遇秋成恨，诚不谬矣。吾今年已二八，未逢折桂之夫；忽慕春情，怎得蟾宫之客？昔日韩夫人得遇于郎[23]，张生偶逢崔氏[24]，曾有《题红记》、《崔徽传》二书。此佳人才子，前以密约偷期[25]，后皆得成秦晋[26]。（长叹介）吾生于宦族，长在名门。年已及笄[27]，不得早成佳配，诚为虚度青春，光阴如过隙耳。（泪介）可惜妾身颜色如花，岂料命如一叶乎！

【山坡羊】没乱里春情难遣[28]，蓦地里怀人幽怨。则为俺生小婵娟，拣名门一例、一例里神仙眷。甚良缘，把青春抛的远！俺的睡情谁见？则索因循腼腆[29]。想幽梦谁边，和春光暗流传？迁延，这衷怀那处言！淹煎，泼残生[30]，除问天！身子困乏了，且自隐几而眠[31]。（睡介）（梦生介）（生持柳枝上）“莺逢日暖歌声滑，人遇风情笑口开。一径落花随水入，今朝阮肇到天台[32]。”小生顺路儿跟着杜小姐回来，怎生不见？（回看介）呀，小姐，小姐！（旦作惊起介）（相见介）（生）小生那一处不寻访小姐来，却在这里！（旦作斜视不语介）（生）恰好花园内，折取垂柳半枝。姐姐，你既淹通书史，可作诗以赏此柳枝乎？（旦作惊喜，欲言又止介）（背想）这生素昧平生，何因到此？（生笑介）小姐，咱爱杀你哩！

【山桃红】则为你如花美眷，似水流年，是答儿闲寻遍[33]。在幽闺自怜。小姐，和你那答儿讲话去。（旦作含笑不行）（生作牵衣介）（旦低问）那边去？（生）转过这芍药栏前，紧靠着湖山石边。（旦低问）秀才，去怎的？（生低答）和你把领扣松，衣带宽，袖梢儿揾着牙儿苫也，则待你忍耐温存一晌眠[34]。（旦作羞）（生前抱）（旦推介）（合）是那处曾相见，相看俨然，早难道这好处相逢无一言[35]？（生强抱旦下）（末扮花神束发冠，红衣插花上）“催花御史惜花天，检点春工又一年。蘸客伤心红雨下[36]，勾人悬梦彩云边。”吾乃掌管南安府后花园花神是也。因杜知府小姐丽娘，与柳梦梅秀才，后日有姻缘之分。杜小姐游春感伤，致使柳秀才入梦。咱花神专掌惜玉怜香，竟来保护他，要他云雨十分欢幸也。

【鲍老催】（末）单则是混阳蒸变，看他似虫儿般蠢动把风情扇。一般儿娇凝翠绽魂儿颠。这是景上缘[37]，想内成，因中见。呀，淫邪展污了花台殿[38]。咱待拈片落花儿惊醒他。（向鬼门丢花介[39]）他梦酣春透了怎留连？拈花闪碎的红如片。秀才才到的半梦儿；梦毕之时，好送杜小姐仍归香阁。吾神去也。（下）

【山桃红】（生、旦携手上）（生）这一霎天留人便，草藉花眠。小姐可好？（旦低头介）（生）则把云鬟点，红松翠偏。小姐休忘了呵，见了你紧相偎，慢厮连，恨不得肉儿般团成片也，逗的个日下胭脂雨上鲜。（旦）秀才，你可去呵？（合）是那处曾相见，相看俨然，早难道这好处相逢无一言？（生）姐姐，你身子乏了，将息，将息。（送旦依前作睡介）（轻拍旦介）姐姐，俺去了。（作回顾介）姐姐，你可十分将息，我再来瞧你那。“行来春色三分雨，睡去巫山一片云。”（下）（旦作惊醒，低叫介）秀才，秀才，你去了也？（又作痴睡介）（老旦上）“夫婿坐黄堂，娇娃立绣窗。怪他裙衩上，花鸟绣双双。”孩儿，孩儿，你为甚瞌睡在此？（旦作醒，叫秀才介）咳也。（老旦）孩儿怎的来？（旦作惊起介）奶奶到此！（老旦）我儿，何不做些针指，或观玩书史，舒展情怀？因何昼寝于此？（旦）孩儿适花园中闲玩，忽值春暄恼人，故此回房。无可消遣，不觉困倦少息。有失迎接，望母亲恕儿之罪。（老旦）孩儿，这后花园中冷静，少去闲行。（旦）领母亲严命。（老旦）孩儿，学堂看书去。（旦）先生不在，且自消停[40]。（老旦叹介）女孩儿长成，自有许多情态，且自由他。正是："宛转随儿女，辛勤做老娘。"（下）（旦长叹介）（看老旦下介）哎也，天那，今日杜丽娘有些侥幸也。偶到后花园中，百花开遍，睹景伤情。没兴而回，昼眠香阁。忽见一生，年可弱冠[41]，丰姿俊妍。于园中折得柳丝一枝，笑对奴家说："姐姐既淹通书史，何不将柳枝题赏一篇？"那时待要应他一声，心中自忖，素昧平生，不知名姓，何得轻与交言。正如此想间，只见那生向前说了几句伤心话儿，将奴搂抱去牡丹亭畔，芍药阑边，共成云雨之欢。两情和合，真个是千般爱惜，万种温存。欢毕之时，又送我睡眠，几声"将息"。正待自送那生出门，忽值母亲来到，唤醒将来。我一身冷汗，乃是南柯一梦[42]。忙身参礼母亲，又被母亲絮了许多闲话。奴家口虽无言答应，心内思想梦中之事，何曾放怀。行坐不宁，自觉如有所失。娘呵，你教我学堂看书去，知他看那一种书消闷也。（作掩泪介）

【绵搭絮】雨香云片[43]，才到梦儿边。无奈高堂，唤醒纱窗睡不便。泼新鲜冷汗粘煎，闪的俺心悠步亸[44]，意软鬟偏。不争多费尽神情[45]，坐起谁饮[46]？则待去眠。（贴上）“晚妆销粉印，春润费香篝[47]。”小姐，薰了被窝睡罢。

【尾声】（旦）困春心游赏倦，也不索香薰绣被眠。天呵，有心情那梦儿还去不远。

春望逍遥出画堂，张　说
间梅遮柳不胜芳。罗　隐
可知刘阮逢人处？许　浑
回首东风一断肠。韦　庄

注 释

[1]乱煞年光遍：缭乱的春光到处都是。

[2]沉烟：沉水香，一种名贵香料。

[3]梅关：即大庾岭，在南安府的南面，宋代在这里设有梅关。

[4]宿妆：隔夜的残妆。

[5]宜春髻子：古时立春那天，妇女剪彩作燕子状，戴在髻上，上贴“宜春”二字。

[6]翦不断，理还乱：语出南唐后主李煜《相见欢》词。

[7]晴丝：游丝，飞丝。

[8]没揣：不意，蓦然。

[9]菱花：镜子。古时用铜镜，背面所铸花纹一般为菱花，因此用菱花代称镜子。

[10]艳晶晶花簪八宝填：镶嵌着多种宝石、光灿灿的簪子。

[11]天然：天性使然。

[12]三春好处：比喻青春美貌。

[13]沉鱼落雁：形容女子美貌。

[14]泥：沾污，这里作动词用。

[15]姹(chà)紫嫣红：花色鲜艳之貌。

[16]锦屏人：深闺中人。

[17]是：凡是、所有的。

[18]啼红了杜鹃：开遍了红色的杜鹃花，这是从杜鹃鸟泣血联想起来的。

[19]缱：留恋、牵绾。

[20]开我西阁门，展我东阁床：语本《木兰诗》："开我东阁门，坐我西阁床。"

[21]映山紫：映山红（杜鹃花）的一种。

[22]宜春面：指新妆。

[23]韩夫人得遇于郎：据唐传奇故事《流红记》，唐僖宗时，宫女韩氏以红叶题诗，从御沟中流出，被于祐拾到。于祐也以红叶题诗，投入沟水的上流，寄给韩氏。后来两人结为夫妇。

[24]张生偶逢崔氏：指张生和崔莺莺的爱情故事，出自唐元稹《会真记》。

[25]偷期：幽会。

[26]得成秦晋：得以结成夫妇。

[27]及笄(jī)：古代女子十五岁开始以笄（簪）束发，叫及笄。

[28]没乱里：形容心绪很乱。

[29]腼腆：害羞。

[30]淹煎，泼残生：淹煎，受熬煎，受折磨：泼残生，苦命。

[31]隐几：靠着几案。

[32]阮肇到天台：用刘晨和阮肇在天台山桃源洞遇见仙女的故事，表示见到爱人。

[33]是答儿：到处。是，凡。下文的“那答儿”指那边。

[34]一晌：一会儿。

[35]早难道：就是难道，但语气较强。

[36]蘸：指红雨（落花）沾在人的身上。

[37]景上缘：景，影；与下文的想、因都是佛家的说法。景上缘，想内成，喻姻缘短暂，如不真实的梦幻。

[38]展污：即沾污、弄脏。

[39]鬼门：一作古门，戏曲舞台上演员上、下场用的门。

[40]消停：休息。

[41]弱冠：二十岁。古代男子到二十岁行冠礼，表示成人。

[42]南柯一梦：唐传奇故事《南柯记》，斜淳于棼梦见被大槐安国国王招为驸马，做南柯太守，历尽富贵荣华和人世浮沉。醒来发现槐安国不过是大槐树下的一个蚁穴，南柯郡即南面树枝下的另一个蚁穴。

[43]雨香云片：指梦中的幽会。

[44]步亸：脚步挪不动。亸，偏斜。

[45]不争多：差不多，几乎。

[46]忺：惬意。

[47]香篝：即薰笼，古代薰香用具。

第三本

第一出 慈 戒

（老旦上）“昨日胜今日，今年老去年[1]。可怜小儿女[2]，长自绣窗前。”几日不到女孩儿房中，午晌去瞧他，只见情思无聊，独眠香阁。问知他在后花园回，身子困倦。他年幼不知：凡少年女子，最不宜艳妆戏游空冷无人之处。这都是春香贱材逗引他。春香那里？（贴上）“闺中图一睡，堂上有千呼。”奶奶，怎夜分时节，还未安寝？（老旦）小姐在那里？（贴）陪过夫人到香阁中，自言自语，淹淹春睡去了[3]。敢在做梦也。（老旦）你这贱材，引逗小姐后花园去。傥有疏虞，怎生是了！（贴）以后再不敢了。（老旦）听俺分付：

【征胡兵】女孩儿只合香闺坐，拈花翦朵。问绣窗针指如何？逗工夫一线多[4]。更昼长闲不过，琴书外自有好腾那[5]。去花园怎么？（贴）花园好景。（老旦）丫头，不说你不知：

【前腔】后花园窣静无边阔[6]，亭台半倒落。便我中年人要去时节，尚兀自里[7]打个磨陀[8]。女儿家甚做作？星辰高犹自可[9]。（贴）不高怎的？（老旦唱）厮撞着，有甚不着科[10]，教娘怎么？小姐不曾晚餐，早饭要早。你说与他。

（老）风雨林中有鬼神，　苏广文
（贴）寂寥未是采花人。　郑　谷
（老）素娥毕竟难防备[11]，段成式
（贴）似有微词动绛唇[12]。唐彦谦

注释

[1]昨日胜今日，今年老去年：见《云溪友议》卷九《艳阳词》所引刘采春唱词。

[2]可怜小儿女：杜甫《月夜》："遥怜小儿女，未解忆长安。"

[3]淹淹：昏昏沉沉。

[4]逗工夫一线多：日子长起来，可以比平日多做一些针线活。一线，刺绣时用完一根线的工夫。《全五代诗》卷十一和凝《宫词百首》："才经冬至阳生后，今日工夫一线多。"

[5]腾那：此作消遣讲。第五本第五出的腾那，却是翻腾、运动的意思。那，同挪。第五本第二出"不见影儿那"，第五本第五出"月影向中那"。

[6]窣静：很静。窣，方言的音写。

[7]尚兀自裹：犹自。

[8]磨陀：徘徊、盘旋，这里作犹豫解。磨陀或作笃么，突磨。

[9]星辰高：迷信的说法，命大、运道好。

[10]有甚不著科：有甚么不对头、出了甚么意外。

[11]素娥：嫦娥，此指杜丽娘。

[12]微词：很婉转的规劝、责备。

第二出 寻 梦

【夜游宫】（贴上）腻脸朝云罢盥，倒犀簪斜插双鬟。侍香闺起早，睡意阑珊[1]：衣桁前[2]，妆阁畔，画屏间。伏侍千金小姐，丫鬟一位春香。请过猫儿师父，不许老鼠放光。侥幸《毛诗》感动，小姐吉日时良。拖带春香遣闷，后花园里游芳。谁知小姐瞌睡，恰遇着夫人问当[3]。絮了小姐一会，要与春香一场[4]。春香无言知罪，以后劝止娘行。夫人还是不放，少不得发咒禁当[5]。（内介）春香姐，发个甚咒来？（贴）敢再跟娘胡撞，教春香即世里不见儿郎[6]。虽然一时抵对，乌鸦管的凤凰？一夜小姐焦躁，起来促水朝妆。由他自言自语，日高花影纱窗。（内介）快请小姐早膳。（贴）"报道官厨饭熟，且去传递茶汤。"（下）

【月儿高】（旦上）几曲屏山展，残眉黛深浅。为甚衾儿里不住的柔肠转？这憔悴非关爱月眠迟倦，可为惜花，朝起庭院？"忽忽花间起梦情，女儿心性未分明。无眠一夜灯明灭，分煞梅香唤不醒[7]。"昨日偶尔春游，何人见梦。绸缪顾盼，如遇平生。独坐思量，情殊怅怳。真个可怜人也。（闷介）（贴捧茶食上）"香饭盛来鹦鹉粒[8]，清茶擎出鹧鸪斑[9]。"小姐早膳哩。（旦）咱有甚心情也！

【前腔】梳洗了才匀面，照台儿未收展[10]。睡起无滋味，茶饭怎生咽？（贴）夫人分付，早饭要早。（旦）你猛说夫人，则待把饥人劝。你说为人在世，怎生叫做吃饭？（贴）一日三餐。（旦）咳，甚瓯儿气力与擎拳！生生的了前件[11]。你自拿去吃便了。（贴）“受用余杯冷炙，胜如剩粉残膏。”（下）（旦）春香已去。天呵，昨日所梦，池亭俨然。只图旧梦重来，其奈新愁一段。寻思展转，竟夜无眠。咱待乘此空闲，背却春香，悄向花园寻看。（悲介）哎也，似咱这般，正是：“梦无彩凤双飞翼，心有灵犀一点通[12]。”（行介）一迳行来，喜的园门洞开，守花的都不在。则这残红满地呵！

【懒画眉】最撩人春色是今年。少什么低就高来粉画垣[13]，元来春心无处不飞悬。（绊介）哎，睡荼蘼抓住裙衩线，恰便是花似人心好处牵。这一湾流水呵！

【前腔】为甚呵，玉真重溯武陵源[14]？也则为水点花飞在眼前。是天公不费买花钱，则咱人心上有啼红怨。咳，辜负了春三二月天。（贴上）吃饭去，不见了小姐，则得一迳寻来。呀，小姐，你在这里！

【不是路】何意婵娟，小立在垂垂花树边[15]。才朝膳，个人无伴怎游园？（旦）画廊前，深深蓦见衔泥燕，随步名园是偶然。（贴）娘回转，幽闺窣地教人见[16]，“那些儿闲串？那些儿闲串[17]？”

【前腔】（旦作恼介）唗，偶尔来前，道的咱偷闲学少年[18]。（贴）咳，不偷闲，偷淡。（旦）欺奴善，把护春台都猜做谎桃源[19]。（贴）敢胡言，这是夫人命，道春多刺绣宜添线，润逼炉香好腻笺[20]。（旦）还说甚来？（贴）这荒园堑，怕花妖木客寻常见[21]。去小庭深院，去小庭深院！（旦）知道了。你好生答应夫人去，俺随后便来。（贴）“闲花傍砌如依主，娇鸟嫌笼会骂人[22]。”（下）（旦）丫头去了，正好寻梦。

【忒忒令】那一答可是湖山石边，这一答似牡丹亭畔。嵌雕阑芍药芽儿浅，一丝丝垂杨线，一丢丢榆荚钱[23]。线儿春甚金钱吊转！呀，昨日那书生将柳枝要我题咏，强我欢会之时，好不话长！

【嘉庆子】是谁家少俊来近远，敢迤逗这香闺去沁园[24]？话到其间腼腆。他捏这眼，奈烦也天[25]；咱噷这口，待酬言。

【尹令】那书生可意呵，咱不是前生爱眷，又素乏平生半面。则道来生出现，乍便今生梦见。生就个书生[26]，恰恰生生抱咱去眠。那些好不动人春意也。

【品令】他倚太湖石，立着咱玉婵娟。待把俺玉山推倒[27]，便日暖玉生烟。捱过雕阑，转过秋千，掯着裙花展[28]。敢席着地，怕天瞧见。好一会分明，美满幽香不可言。梦到正好时节，甚花片儿吊下来也！

【豆叶黄】他兴心儿紧咽咽[29]，呜着咱香肩[30]。俺可也慢掂掂做意儿周旋[31]。等闲间把一个照人儿昏善，那般形现，那般软绵[32]。忑一片撒花心的红影儿吊将来半天[33]。敢是咱梦魂儿厮缠？咳，寻来寻去，都不见了。牡丹亭，芍药阑，怎生这般凄凉冷落，杳无人迹？好不伤心也！

【玉交枝】（泪介）是这等荒凉地面，没多半亭台靠边，好是咱眯睽色眼寻难见[34]。明放着白日青天，猛教人抓不到魂梦前。霎时间有如活现，打方旋再得俄延[35]，呀，是这答儿压黄金钏匾[36]。要再见那书生呵，

【月上海棠】怎赚骗，依稀想像人儿见。那来时荏苒[37]，去也迁延。非远，那雨迹云踪才一转，敢依花傍柳还重现。昨日今朝，眼下心前，阳台一座登时变。再消停一番。（望介）呀，无人之处，忽然大梅树一株，梅子磊磊可爱。

【二犯幺令】偏则他暗香清远，伞儿般盖的周全。他趁这，

他趁这春三月红绽雨肥天[38]，叶儿青，偏迸着苦仁儿里撒圆[39]。爱杀这昼阴便，再得到罗浮梦边[40]。罢了，这梅树依依可人，我杜丽娘若死后，得葬于此，幸矣。

【江儿水】偶然间心似缱，梅树边。这般花花草草由人恋，生生死死随人愿，便酸酸楚楚无人怨[41]。待打并香魂一片[42]，阴雨梅天，守的个梅根相见。（倦坐介）（贴上）"佳人拾翠春亭远[43]，侍女添香午院清。"咳，小姐走乏了，梅树下眂。

【川拨棹】你游花院，怎靠着梅树偃？（旦）一时间望，一时间望眼连天，忽忽地伤心自怜。（泣介）（合）知怎生情怅然，知怎生泪暗悬？（贴）小姐甚意儿？

【前腔】（旦）春归人面，整相看无一言，我待要折，我待要折的那柳枝儿问天，我如今悔，我如今悔不与题笺。（贴）这一句猜头儿是怎言[44]？（合前）（贴）去罢。（旦作行又住介）

【前腔】为我慢归休，缓留连。（内鸟啼介）听，听这不如归春暮天[45]，难道我再，难道我再到这亭园，则挣的个长眠和短眠[46]！（合前）（贴）到了，和小姐瞧奶奶去。（旦）罢了。

【意不尽】软咍咍刚扶到画阑偏[47]，报堂上夫人稳便。咱杜丽娘呵，少不得楼上花枝也则是照独眠。

（旦）武陵何处访仙郎？释皎然

（贴）只怪游人思易忘。韦庄

（旦）从此时时春梦里，白居易

（贴）一生遗恨系心肠。张祜

注释

[1]阑珊：衰残，这里是尚未消退的意思。

[2]衣桁(héng)：衣架。

[3]问当：就是问，当是语助词。

[4]一场：这里指打一场或骂一场。

[5]禁当：禁也就是当，这里是抵对、对付的意思。

[6]即世里不见儿郎：这辈子嫁不到丈夫。

[7]分：同忿。

[8]鹦鹉粒：饭食，语出杜甫《秋兴》八首中诗句“香稻啄余鹦鹉粒”。

[9]鹧鸪斑：形容盏中的茶影。

[10]照台儿：镜台。

[11]甚瓯儿气力与擎拳！生生的了前件：哪有气力捧碗吃饭！勉强算吃过了。

[12]梦无彩凤双飞翼，心有灵犀一点通：出自唐李商隐《无题》诗，原诗“梦”作“身”。

[13]少什么：多的是。全句意思是说，重重的粉墙关不住满园春色。

[14]玉真重溯武陵源：比喻自己到花园来寻梦。

[15]垂垂花树：指梅花。

[16]猝：同猝。

[17]那些儿闲串：哪儿乱跑？

[18]道的咱偷闲学少年：宋程颢诗《春日偶成》：“时人不识余心乐，将谓偷闲学少年。”

[19]护春台：这里指花园。

[20]腻：使纸张更加滑润。

[21]见：同现。

[22]娇鸟嫌笼会骂人：唐李山甫《公子家》二首中诗句：“鹦鹉嫌笼解骂人。”

[23]一丢丢：一串串。

[24]迤逗这香闺去沁园：逗引我到花园里去。

[25]他捏这眼，奈烦也天：他捏这眼，这是回忆梦中幽会时男子对她的抚爱。奈烦也天，极言男子对她温柔体贴，百般爱惜。下文的“噷”，意为动、开。

[26]生：勉强，半推半就。

[27]玉山：指身体。

[28]揹：把持、勒住。

[29]兴心儿：着意。

[30]呜：吻，吮嘬。

[31]慢惦惦：慢吞吞。

[32]“等闲间把一个照人儿昏善”三句：轻易地把一个明白的人弄得这般昏迷软善。

[33]忑(tè)：受惊。

[34]好是：正是。

[35]打方旋：盘旋，徘徊。

[36]匾：扁。

[37]荏苒：时间慢慢过去。

[38]红绽雨肥天：指梅子成熟的时候。

[39]偏迸着苦仁儿里撒圆：梅子是圆的，它的果仁是苦的。仁，双关人。全句意谓怨梅子偏在她这个苦命的人面前结得圆圆的。

[40]再得到罗浮梦边：意指能和柳梦梅在梦里再相会。

[41]“这般花花草草由人恋”三句：如果想爱什么就爱什么：生死都由自己决定，那么就算哭哭啼啼，也不会怨天尤命了。

[42]打并：拚着。

[43]拾翠：拾取翠鸟的羽毛，这里指游园。

[44]猜头儿：谜。

[45]不如归：“不如归去”，拟杜鹃鸟的啼声。

[46]“难道我再到这亭园”两句：难道除了梦中（短眠）和死后（长眠），我就不能再到这亭园里来吗？

[47]软咍咍：软绵绵。

第三出 诀谒

【杏花天】（生上）虽然是饱学名儒，腹中饥，峥嵘胀气[1]。梦魂中紫阁丹墀[2]，猛抬头、破屋半间而已。“蛟龙失水砚池枯，狡兔腾天笔势孤[3]。百事不成真画虎，一枝难稳又惊乌[4]。”我柳梦梅在广州学里，也是个数一数二的秀才，捱了些数伏数九的日子[5]。于今藏身荒圃，寄口髯奴[6]。思之、思之，惶愧、惶愧。想起韩友之谈，不如外县傍州，寻觅活计。正是：“家徒四壁求杨意[7]，树少千头愧木奴[8]。”老园公那里？

【字字双】（净扮郭驼上）前山低坬后山堆[9]，驼背；牵弓射弩做人儿，把势[10]；一连十个偌来回[11]，漏地[12]；有时跌做绣球儿，滚气。自家种园的郭驼子是也。祖公公郭橐驼，从唐朝柳员外来柳州。我因兵乱，跟随他二十八代玄孙柳梦梅秀才的父亲，流转到广，又是若干年矣。卖果子回来，看秀才去。（见介）秀才，读书辛苦。（生）园公，正待商量一事。我读书过了廿岁，并无发迹之期。思想起来，前路多长，岂能郁郁居此。搬柴运水，多有劳累。园中果树，都判与伊[13]。听我道来：

【桂花锁南枝】俺有身如寄，无人似你。俺吃尽了黄淡酸甜[14]，费你老人家浇培接植。你道俺像甚的来？镇日里似醉汉扶头[15]。甚日的和老驼伸背？自株守[16]，教怨谁？让荒园，你存济[17]。

【前腔】（净）俺橐驼风味，种园家世。（揖介）不能勾展脚伸腰，也和你鞠躬尽力。秀才，你贴了俺果园那里去？（生）坐食三餐，不如走空一棍。（净）怎生叫做一棍？（生）混名打秋风哩[18]！（净）咳，你费工夫去撞府穿州[19]，不如依本分登科及第。（生）你说打秋风不好？"茂陵刘郎秋风客[20]"，到大来做了皇帝[21]。（净）秀才，不要攀今吊古的。你待秋风谁？你道滕王阁，风顺随[22]，则怕鲁颜碑，响雷碎[23]。（生）俺干谒之兴甚浓，休的阻挡[24]。（净）也整理些衣服去。

【尾声】把破衫衿彻骨捶挑洗。（生）学干谒黉门一布衣。（净）秀才，则要你衣锦还乡俺还见的你。

（生）此身飘泊苦西东，　杜　甫
（净）笑指生涯树树红。　陆龟蒙
（生）欲尽出游那可得？　武元衡
（净）秋风还不及春风[25]。王　建

注释

[1]峥嵘：本是形容山势高峻，这里指一肚子闷气。

[2]紫阁丹墀：宫殿，指在朝廷为官。

[3]狡兔腾天笔势孤：兔毫是制毛笔的原料。狡兔腾天，则没有毫毛，所以笔势孤。

[4]一枝难稳又惊乌：以惊乌比喻自己找不到栖身之所。上句画虎用汉马援《诫兄子严、敦书》："所谓画虎不成，反类狗者也。"

[5]数伏数九：酷暑和严寒。

[6]寄口髯奴：倚靠奴仆为生。

[7]求杨意：指求人荐引。杨意，汉代杨得意，将司马相如推荐给汉武帝。

[8]树少千头愧木奴：果树少，不能维持生活。木奴，指橘树，语本《三国志》裴注引《襄阳记》中李衡故事。

[9]前山低𡉏(guà)后山堆：形容腹部凹下、背部隆起的样子。

[10]把势：装样子。

[11]偌：这样。

[12]漏地：走不快，走不稳。漏地，一作漏蹄，原是骡马的一种蹄病。

[13]判：给予。

[14]黄：黄齑，咸菜。

[15]扶头：形容醉态。

[16]自株守：自己不出去想办法。

[17]存济：存活，过生活。

[18]秋风：也作抽丰，指利用各种关系向人索要钱物。

[19]撞府穿州：在外地东奔西跑。

[20]茂陵刘郎秋风客：语出唐李贺《金铜仙人辞汉歌》。茂陵，汉武帝的陵墓；刘郎，指武帝。秋风，原是说像汉武帝那样不可一世的人，生命也一样短促，好像秋风中的过客。这里是双关打秋风。

[21]到大来：倒、反而。

[22]滕王阁，风顺随：指运道好。传说有神相助唐王勃，一夜间赶到七八百里之外的滕王阁，写下千古名篇《滕王阁序》。

[23]鲁颜碑，响雷碎：指运气坏。传说宋代张镐贫寒，荐福寺僧想拓印颜真卿（封鲁郡公，世称颜鲁公）所书碑文资助它，结果石碑当夜被雷击毁。

[24]休的：休得。

[25]秋风还不及春风：意谓打秋风不如考试及第。

第四出 写 真

【破齐阵】（旦上）径曲梦回人杳，闺深佩冷魂销。似雾濛花，如云漏月，一点幽情动早。（贴上）怕待寻芳迷翠蝶，倦起临妆听伯劳[1]。春归红袖招。**【醉桃源】**“（旦）不经人事意相关，牡丹亭梦残。（贴）断肠春色在眉弯，倩谁临远山[2]？（旦）排恨叠，怯衣单，花枝红泪弹[3]。（合）蜀妆晴雨画来难[4]，高唐云影间。”（贴）小姐，你自花园游后，寝食悠悠，敢为春伤，顿成消瘦？春香愚不谏贤，那花园以后再不可行走了。（旦）你怎知就里？这是：“春梦暗随三月景，晓寒瘦减一分花。”

【刷子序犯】（旦低唱）春归恁寒悄，都来[5]几日意懒心乔[6]，竟妆成熏香独坐无聊。逍遥，怎刬尽助愁芳草，甚法儿点活心苗[7]！真情强笑为谁娇？泪花儿打迸着梦魂飘。

【朱奴儿犯】（贴）小姐，你热性儿怎不冰着，冷泪儿几曾干燥？这两度春游忒分晓，是禁不的燕抄莺闹[8]。你自窨约[9]，敢夫人见焦[10]。再愁烦，十分容貌怕不上九分瞧。（旦作惊介）咳，听春香言话，俺丽娘瘦到九分九了。俺且镜前一照，委是如何[11]？（照介）（悲介）哎也，俺往日艳冶轻盈，奈何一瘦至此！若不趁此时自行描画，流在人间，一旦无常[12]，谁知西蜀杜丽娘有如此之美貌乎！春香，取素绢、丹青，看我描画。（贴下取绢、笔上）“三分春色描来易，一段伤心画出难。”绢幅、丹青，俱已齐备。（旦泣介）杜丽娘二八春容[13]，怎生便是杜丽娘自手生描也呵！

【普天乐】这些时把少年人如花貌，不多时憔悴了。不因他福分难销，可甚的红颜易老？论人间绝色偏不少，等把风光丢抹早[14]。打灭起离魂舍[15]欲火三焦[16]，摆列着昭容阁文房四宝[17]，待画出西子湖眉月双高[18]。

【雁过声】（照镜叹介）轻绡，把镜儿擘掠[19]。笔花尖淡扫轻描。影儿呵，和你细评度[20]：你腮斗儿恁喜谑[21]，则待注樱桃[22]，染柳条[23]，渲云鬟烟霭飘萧[24]；眉梢青未了，个中人全在秋波妙[25]，可可的淡春山钿翠小[26]。

【倾杯序】（贴）宜笑，淡东风立细腰，又似被春愁着。（旦）谢半点江山，三分门户，一种人才，小小行乐，捻青梅闲厮调。倚湖山梦晓[27]，对垂杨风袅。忒苗条，斜添他几叶翠芭蕉。春香，幪起来[28]，可厮像也？

【玉芙蓉】（贴）丹青女易描，真色人难学[29]。似空花水月[30]，影儿相照。（旦喜介）画的来可爱人也。咳，情知画到中间好，再有似生成别样娇。（贴）只少个姐夫在身傍。若是姻缘早，把风流婿招，少什么美夫妻图画在碧云高！（旦）春香，咱不瞒你，花园游玩之时，咱也有个人儿。（贴惊介）小姐，怎的有这等方便呵？（旦）梦哩！

【山桃犯】有一个曾同笑，待想象生描着，再消详邈入其中妙[31]，则女孩家怕漏泄风情稿。这春容呵，似孤秋片月离云峤，甚蟾宫贵客傍的云霄[32]？春香，记起来了。那梦里书生，曾折柳一枝赠我。此莫非他日所适之夫姓柳乎？故有此警报耳[33]。偶成一诗，暗藏春色，题于帧首之上何如？（贴）却好。（旦题吟介）“近睹分明似俨然，远观自在若飞仙。他年得傍蟾宫客，不在梅边在柳边。”（放笔叹介）春香，也有古今美女，早嫁了丈夫相爱，替他描模画样；也有美人自家写照，寄与情人。似我杜丽娘寄谁呵！

【尾犯序】心喜转心焦。喜的明妆俨雅，仙佩飘飖。则怕呵，把俺年深色浅，当了个金屋藏娇[34]。虚劳，寄春容教谁泪落，做真真无人唤叫。（泪介）堪愁夭，精神出现留与后人标[35]。春香，悄悄唤那花郎分付他。（贴叫介）（丑扮花郎上）“秦宫一生花里活[36]，崔徽不似卷中人[37]。”小姐有何分付？（旦）这一幅行乐图，向行家裱去[38]。叫人家收拾好些。

【鲍老催】这本色人儿妙，助美的谁家裱？要练[39]花绡帘儿莹[40]、边阑小，教他有人问着休胡嘌[41]。日炙风吹悬衬的好，怕好物不坚牢。把咱巧丹青休涴了。（丑）小姐，裱完了，安奉在那里？

【尾声】（旦）尽香闺赏玩无人到，（贴）这形模则合挂巫山庙。（合）又怕为雨为云飞去了。

（贴）眼前珠翠与心违，　崔道融
（旦）却向花前痛哭归。　韦　庄
（贴）好写妖娆与教看，　罗　虬
（旦）令人评泊画杨妃[42]。韩　偓

注释

[1]伯劳：一名鵙，鸣禽类。

[2]临远山：指画眉毛。远山，眉毛的一种式样。

[3]红泪：指花上的露水。这里杜丽娘以花自喻。

[4]蜀妆：指巫山神女。

[5]都来：算来。

[6]心乔：心绪不好。

[7]逍遥，怎刬尽助愁芳草，甚法儿点活心苗：怎么才能除尽助愁的芳草，点活心苗，获得逍遥自在。刬，同铲。

[8]抄：同吵。

[9]窨约：思忖。

[10]敢夫人见焦：恐怕夫人焦心。

[11]委是：果然是，真的是。

[12]无常：对死的隐讳说法。

[13]春容：青春的容颜。

[14]等把风光丢抹早：都很早就容颜衰减。

[15]离魂舍：躯壳，佛家语。

[16]欲火三焦：凡俗之情。佛家说有三欲，形貌欲、姿态欲、细触欲，一作饮食欲、睡眠欲、淫欲。三焦，原来是道家和中医用语，这里是借用。

[17]昭容阁：内宫。昭容，妃嫔之类宫中女官。

[18]西子湖眉月：西子湖，比西施；眉月，比眉毛。

[19]擘掠：揩拭。

[20]评度(duò)：评论。

[21]腮斗儿：颊。

[22]注樱桃：画朱唇。

[23]染柳条：画眉毛。

[24]烟霭飘萧：形容头发。

[25]个中人：此中人，这里指画中人。

[26]可可的：恰恰的。

[27]倚湖山梦晓：此句以下也是写杜丽娘自画像中的姿态。

[28]幁：同帧，张开画幅。

[29]真色：佛家语，这里意近于下文所说“本色”。

[30]空花水月：形容真色难以捉摸。

[31]再消详邈入其中妙：再慢慢地把他的神情描入画中。邈，同描。

[32]甚蟾宫贵客傍的云霄：谁能和画中的美人挨在一起呢？蟾宫贵客，指新考中的进士。

[33]警报：预兆。

[34]则怕呵，把俺年深色浅，当了个金屋藏娇：只怕这张画老是藏着，年深月久，连色彩也褪了。

[35]标：品题、鉴赏。

[36]秦宫：东汉大将军梁冀所宠幸的监奴名，这里是花郎自指。

[37]崔徽不似卷中人：意思是说人消瘦了。宋人所编笔记小说集《丽情集》中《崔徽传》，妓女崔徽托人将画像带给情人，说自己已不像画中人那样美丽，将要死了。

[38]行家：专业匠人，这里指裱画店。

[39]练：织物煮熟漂白叫练，这里作形容词用。

[40]帘儿：裱好的画幅上方的空白。

[41]胡嘌：胡说。

[42]评泊：评说。

第四本

第一出 诘 病

【三登乐】（老旦上）今生怎生？偏则是红颜薄命，眼见的孤苦仃俜。（泣介）掌上珍，心头肉，泪珠儿暗倾。天呵，偏人家七子团圆[1]，一个女孩儿厮病[2]。（清平乐）“如花娇怯，合得天饶借[3]。风雨于花生分劣[4]，作意十分凌藉。止堪深阁重帘，谁教月榭风檐[5]。我发短回肠寸断，眼昏眵泪双淹[6]。”老身年将半百，单生一女丽娘。因何一病，起倒半年[7]？看他举止容谈，不似风寒暑湿。中间缘故，春香必知，则问他便了。春香贱才那里？（贴上）有哩。我“眼里不逢乖小使[8]，掌中擎着个病多娇。得知堂上夫人召，剩酒残脂要咱消”。春香叩头。（老旦）小姐闲常好好的，才着你贱才伏侍他，不上半年，偏是病害。可恼，可恼！且问近日茶饭多少？

【驻马听】（贴）他茶饭何曾，所事儿休提、叫懒应。看他娇啼隐忍，笑谵迷厮[9]，睡眼懵憕[10]。（老旦）早早禀请太医了[11]。（贴）则除是八法针针断软绵情[12]。怕九还丹[13]丹不的腌臜证[14]。（老旦）是什么病？（贴）春香不知，道他一枕秋清，却怎生还害的是春前病。（老旦哭介）怎生了。

【前腔】他一搦身形[15]，瘦的庞儿没了四星[16]。都是小奴才逗他。大古是烟花惹事[17]，莺燕成招，云月知情。贱才还不跪！取家法来。（贴跪介）春香实不知道。（老旦）因何瘦坏了玉娉婷，你怎生触损了他娇情性？（贴）小姐好好的拈花弄柳，不知因甚病了。（老旦恼，打贴介）打你这牢承[18]，嘴骨棱的胡遮映[19]。（贴）夫人休闪了手[20]。容春香诉来。便是那一日游花园回来，夫人撞到时节，说个秀才手里折的柳枝儿，要小姐题诗。小姐说这秀才素昧平生，也不和他题了。（老旦）不题罢了。后来？（贴）后来那、那、那秀才就一拍手把小姐端端正正抱在牡丹亭上去了。（老旦）去怎的？（贴）春香怎得知？小姐做梦哩。（老旦惊介）是梦么？（贴）是梦。（老旦）这等着鬼了。快请老爷商议。（贴请介）老爷有请。（外上）"肘后印嫌金带重[21]，掌中珠怕玉盘轻[22]。"夫人，女儿病体因何？（老旦泣介）老爷听讲：

【前腔】说起心疼，这病知他是怎生！看他长眠短起，似笑如啼，有影无形[23]。原来女儿到后花园游了。梦见一人手执柳枝，闪了他去[24]。（作叹介）怕腰身触污了柳精灵，虚嚣侧犯了花神圣[25]。老爷呵，急与禳星[26]，怕流星赶月相刑迸[27]。（外）却还来。我请陈斋长教书，要他拘束身心。你为母亲的，倒纵他闲游。（笑介）则是些日炙风吹，伤寒流转。便要禳解，不用师巫，则叫紫阳宫石道婆诵些经卷可矣。古语云："信巫不信医，一不治也。"我已请过陈斋长看他脉息去了。（老旦）看甚脉息。若早有了人家，敢没这病。（外）咳，古者男子三十而娶，女子二十而嫁[28]。女儿点点年纪，知道个什么呢？

【前腔】忒恁憨生[29]，一个哇儿甚七情[30]？则不过往来潮热，大小伤寒，急慢风惊[31]。则是你为母的呵，真珠不放在掌中擎，因此娇花不奈这心头病。（泣介）（合）两口丁零[32]，告天天，半边儿是咱全家命[33]。

柳起东风惹病身， 李　绅
举家相对却沾巾。 刘长卿
遍依仙法多求药， 张　籍
念见蓬山不死人。 项　斯

注释

[1]七子团圆：祝颂用的成语。
[2]厮病：害病。
[3]饶借：宽免、怜惜。
[4]生分劣：作恶。生分，即生忿，与人过不去。
[5]月榭风檐：月下风前的亭台。这里指《惊梦》一出中所写的游园。
[6]眵(chī)：眼睛分泌出来的黏液。
[7]起倒：好一阵坏一阵，轻一阵重一阵，久病不愈。
[8]乖小使：乖，伶俐乖巧；小使，书童之类当差的男孩。
[9]迷厮：形容精神恍惚。
[10]懵懂：懵懂，神志模糊，这里是形容睡眼朦胧。
[11]太医：御医，这里泛指一般医师。
[12]八法针：犹言最好的针刺医术。
[13]九还丹：即九转丹，道家所炼的一种金丹，据说吃了可以成仙。
[14]腌臜证：骯髒病，相思病的代称。
[15]一搦：一捻，形容腰身纤细。
[16]瘦的庞儿没有四星：瘦得不成样子。四星，秤杆末尾钉有四星，易磨灭。

[17]大古是：总是。

[18]牢承：原作殷勤解，这里指滑头、善于献殷勤的人。

[19]嘴骨稜：指多言多语。

[20]闪：扭伤。

[21]肘后印嫌金带重：形容年老倦于居官。

[22]掌中珠怕玉盘轻：怕女儿养不大。

[23]有影无形：指病情。

[24]闪：这里是引的意思。

[25]虚嚣侧犯了花神圣：虚弱（虚嚣）的身子触犯（侧犯）花神。侧犯，比正犯情节较轻。

[26]禳星：禳，道教说法，用符咒为人去邪除病。

[27]流星赶月相刑迸：星命家的说法。流星赶月，就是有冲破。刑，如子卯相刑，比相冲的情节较轻；迸，拚，冲克。刑、迸，主凶事，这里用迷信说法推究病因。

[28]古者男子三十而娶，女子二十而嫁：语出《礼记•内则》。

[29]忒恁憨生：那样娇憨的样子，形容少女还不懂事。

[30]一个哇儿甚七情：哇，娃。七情，喜、怒、哀、惧、爱、恶、欲，这里特指男女之情。

[31]往来潮热，大小伤寒，急慢风惊：潮热、伤寒、急慢惊风都是疾病的名称。急惊风，小儿急症；慢惊风，脑膜炎之类的病；伤寒，中医所指的伤寒和西医不同。

[32]丁零：零丁，孤单。

[33]半边儿：女婿称半子，这里指女儿。

第二出 诊 祟

【一江风】（贴扶病旦上）（旦）病迷厮。为甚轻憔悴？打不破愁魂谜。梦初回，燕尾翻风，乱飒起湘帘翠。春去偌多时，春去偌多时，花容只顾衰。井梧声刮的我心儿碎。（行香子）春香啊，我“楚楚精神，叶叶腰身，能禁多病逡巡[1]！（贴）你星星措与[2]，种种生成，有许多娇，许多韵，许多情。（旦）咳，咱弄梅心事[3]，那折柳情人[4]，梦淹渐暗老残春。（贴）正好簟炉香午，枕扇风清。知为谁颦，为谁瘦，为谁疼？”（旦）春香，我自春游一梦，卧病如今。不痒不疼，如痴如醉。知他怎生？（贴）小姐，梦儿里事，想他则甚！（旦）你教我怎生不想啊！

【金落索】贪他半晌痴，赚了多情泥[5]。待不思量，怎不思量得？就里暗销肌，怕人知。嗽腔腔嫩喘微[6]。哎哟，我这惯淹煎的样子谁怜惜？自噤窄的春心怎的支[7]？心儿悔，悔当初一觉留春睡。（贴）老夫人替小姐冲喜[8]。（旦）信他冲的个甚喜？到的年时，敢犯杀花园内[9]？

【前腔】（贴）看他春归何处归，春睡何曾睡？气丝儿怎度的长天日？把心儿捧凑眉，病西施[10]。小姐，梦去知他实实谁？病来只送的个虚虚的你。做行云先渴倒在巫阳会[11]。全无谓，把单相思害得忒明昧[12]。又不是困人天气，中酒心期[13]，魆魆地常如醉[14]。（末上）“日下晒书嫌鸟迹，月中捣药要蟾酥[15]。”我陈最良承公相命，来诊视小姐脉息。到此后堂，不免打叫一声。春香贤弟有么？（贴见介）是陈师父。小姐睡哩。（末）免惊动他。我自进去。（见介）小姐。（旦作惊介）谁？（贴）陈师父哩。（旦扶起介）（旦）师父，我学生患病。久失敬了。（末）学生，学生，古书有云："学精于勤，荒于嬉[16]。"你因为后花园汤风冒日[17]，感下这疾，荒废书工。我为师的在外，寝食不安。幸喜老公相请来看病。也不料你清减至此。似这般样，几时能勾起来读书？早则端阳节哩。（贴）师父，端节有你的。（末）我说端阳，难道要你粽子？小姐，望闻问切[18]，我且问你病症因何？（贴）师父问什么！只因你讲《毛诗》，这病便是"君子好求"上来的。（末）是那一位君子？（贴）知他是那一位君子。（末）这般说，《毛诗》病用《毛诗》去医。那头一卷就有女科圣惠方在里[19]。（贴）师父，可记的《毛诗》上方儿？（末）便依他处方。小姐害了"君子"的病，用的史君子[20]。《毛诗》："既见君子，云胡不瘳？[21]"这病有了君子抽一抽，就抽好了。（旦羞介）哎也！（贴）还有甚药？（末）酸梅十个。《诗》云："摽有梅，其实七兮[22]"，又说："其实三兮。"三个打七个，是十个。此方单医男女过时思酸之病。（旦叹介）（贴）还有呢？（末）天南星三个[23]。（贴）可少？（末）再添些。《诗》云："三星在天。[24]"专医男女及时之病。（贴）还有呢？（末）俺看小姐一肚子火，你可抹净一个大马桶，待我用栀子仁、当归，泻下他火来。这也是依方："之子于归，言秣其马。"（贴）师父，这马不同那"其马"。（末）一样髀鞦窟洞下。（旦）好个伤风切药陈先生。（贴）做的按月通经陈妈妈。（旦）师父不可执方[25]，还是诊脉为稳。（末看脉，错按旦手背介）（贴）师父，讨个转手。（末）女人反此背看之，正是王叔和《脉诀》[26]。也罢，顺手看是。（诊脉介）呀，小姐脉息，到这个分际了。

【金索挂梧桐】他人才忒整齐，脉息恁微细。小小香闺，为甚伤憔悴？（起介）春香啊，似他这伤春怯夏肌，好扶持。病烦人容易伤秋意。小姐，我去咀药来[27]。（旦叹介）师父，少不得情栽了窍髓针难入[28]，病躲在烟花你药怎知[29]？（泣介）承尊觑，何时何日来看这女颜回[30]？（合）病中身怕的是惊疑。且将息，休烦絮。（旦）师父且自在。送不得你了。可曾把俺八字推算么？（末）算来要过中秋好。“当生止有八个字[31]，起死曾无三世医[32]。”（下）

（贴）绿惨双蛾不自持，　步非烟
（净）道家妆束厌禳时[33]。薛　能
（旦）如今不在花红处，　僧怀济
（合）为报东风且莫吹。　李　涉

注释

[1]多病逡巡：久病。逡巡，徘徊不去，这里指疾病缠绵。

[2]星星措与：星星，件件。措与，举措、行事。

[3]弄梅心事：这里指杜丽娘怀春的心事。

[4]折柳情人：指柳梦梅。

[5]赚了多情泥：赚，骗取。这里是害得、弄得的意思。泥，与“撒滞腻”的“腻”通，意谓为感情所牵缠。

[6]腔腔：象声词，咳嗽的声音。

[7]噤窄：闷在心里，有心事不对人说。

[8]冲喜：迷信说法，以办喜事去冲破即将发生的凶事。

[9]到的年时，敢犯杀花园内：难道是从前（年时）在花园里冲撞了什么神道？以疑问句表示否定的意义。到的，道的、想是的意思。

[10]把心儿捧凑眉，病西施：西施，春秋时代越国美女，据说她犯心疼病时捧心颦眉，样子很美。

[11]巫阳：巫山之阳（南）。

[12]明昧：不明不白。

[13]心期：本意是向往，这里作心绪讲。

[14]魆魆地：精神恍惚貌。

[15]月中捣药要蟾酥：神话传说，月亮里有白兔捣药。蟾酥，蟾蜍皮疣内毒腺的分泌液，供药用。

[16]学精于勤，荒于嬉：唐韩愈《进学解》中的句子。

[17]汤风：冒风，受了风吹。

[18]望、闻、问、切：中医诊病的四种方法。

[19]圣惠方：灵验的处方。

[20]史君子：应作使君子，中药名。

[21]既见君子，云胡不瘳(chōu)：语出《诗•郑风•风雨》。君子，《风雨》这首诗中少女的爱人；云，语助词，无义，胡，为什么；瘳，病愈。

[22]摽有梅，其实七兮：语出《诗•召南•摽有梅》，意思是梅子落下来了，树上还留着七个。

[23]天南星：中药名。

[24]三星在天：三星，心宿，傍晚出现在东方。语出《诗经•唐风•绸缪》。

[25]执方：固执。

[26]王叔和《脉诀》：王叔和，晋代著名医学家，著有《脉经》《脉诀》《脉赋》。

[27]咀药：中药中的一些药材，按照旧法，煎煮前要用嘴嚼细。这里作煎药解。

[28]情栽了窍髓针难入：意思是相思的病根生在骨髓里面，针刺不进去。

[29]烟花：犹言风月，指情爱。

[30]女颜回：指优秀而短命的女学生。颜回是孔子最满意的弟子。

[31]八个字：八字，星命家根据人出生的年、月、日、时所配的干支共八个字推算其命运。

[32]三世医：祖传三代的医生。

[33]厌禳：厌、禳都是禳解的意思。

第三出 闹殇

【金珑璁】（贴上）连宵风雨重，多娇多病愁中。仙少效，药无功。“颦有为颦，笑有为笑[1]。不颦不笑，哀哉年少。”春香侍奉小姐，伤春病到深秋。今夕中秋佳节，风雨萧条。小姐病转沉吟，待我扶他消遣。正是：“从来雨打中秋月，更值风摇长命灯[2]。”（下）

【鹊桥仙】（贴扶病旦上）拜月堂空，行云径拥，骨冷怕成秋梦。世间何物似情浓？整一片断魂心痛。（旦）“枕函敲破漏声残[3]，似醉如呆死不难。一段暗香迷夜雨，十分清瘦怯秋寒。”春香，病境沉沉，不知今夕何夕？（贴）八月半了。（旦）哎也，是中秋佳节哩。老爷，奶奶，都为我愁烦，不曾玩赏了？（贴）这都不在话下了。（旦）听见陈师父替我推命，要过中秋。看看病势转沉，今宵欠好。你为我开轩一望，月色如何？（贴开窗，旦望介）

【集贤宾】（旦）海天悠、问冰蟾何处涌[4]？玉杵秋空，凭谁窃药把嫦娥奉？甚西风吹梦无踪！人去难逢，须不是神挑鬼弄。在眉峰，心坎里别是一般疼痛[5]。（旦闷介）

【前腔】（贴）甚春归无端厮和哄[6]，雾和烟两不玲珑[7]。算来人命关天重，会消详、直恁匆匆！为着谁侬[8]，俏样子等闲抛送？待我谎他。姐姐，月上了。月轮空，敢蘸破你一床幽梦[9]。（旦望叹介）“轮时盼节想中秋，人到中秋不自由。奴命不中孤月照，残生今夜雨中休。”

【前腔】你便好中秋月儿谁受用？剪西风泪雨梧桐[10]。楞生瘦骨加沉重[11]。趱程期是那天外哀鸿[12]。草际寒蛩，撒刺刺纸条窗缝。（旦惊作昏介）冷松松，软兀刺四梢难动[13]。（贴惊介）小姐冷厥了。夫人有请。（老旦上）“百岁少忧夫主贵，一生多病女儿娇。”我的儿，病体怎生了？（贴）奶奶，欠好，欠好。（老旦）可怎了！

【前腔】不堤防你后花园闲梦铳[14]，不分明再不惺忪[15]，睡临侵[16]打不起头梢重[17]。（泣介）恨不呵早早乘龙[18]。夜夜孤鸿，活害杀俺翠娟娟雏凤。一场空，是这答里把娘儿命送。

【啭林莺】（旦醒介）甚飞丝缱的阳神动[19]，弄悠扬风马叮咚[20]。（泣介）娘，儿拜谢你了。（拜跌介）从小来觑的千金重，不孝女孝顺无终。娘呵，此乃天之数也。当今生花开一红，愿来生把萱椿再奉。（众泣介）（合）恨西风，一霎无端碎绿摧红。

【前腔】（老旦）并无儿、荡得个娇香种[21]，绕娘前笑眼欢容。但成人索把俺高堂送[22]。恨天涯老运孤穷。儿呵，暂时间月直年空[23]，返将息你这心烦意冗。（合前）（旦）娘，你女儿不幸，作何处置？（老旦）奔你回去也[24]。儿！

【玉莺儿】（旦泣介）旅榇[25]梦魂中，盼家山千万重。（老旦）便远也去。（旦）是不是[26]，听女孩儿一言。这后园中一株梅树，儿心所爱。但葬我梅树之下可矣。（老旦）这是怎的来？（旦）做不的病婵娟桂窟里长生[27]，则分的粉骷髅向梅花古洞[28]。（老旦泣介）看他强扶头泪濛，冷淋心汗倾，不如我先他一命无常用。（合）恨苍穹，妒花风雨，偏在月明中。（老旦）还去与爹讲，广做道场也。儿，“银蟾谩捣君臣药[29]，纸马重烧子母钱[30]。”（下）（旦）春香，咱可有回生之日否？

【前腔】（叹介）你生小事依从，我情中你意中。春香，你小心奉事老爷奶奶。（贴）这是当的了。（旦）春香，我记起一事来。我那春容，题诗在上，外观不雅。葬我之后，盛着紫檀匣儿，藏在太湖石底。（贴）这是主何意儿？（旦）有心灵翰墨春容，傥直那人知重[31]。（贴）姐姐宽心。你如今不幸，坟孤独影。肯将息起来，禀过老爷，但是姓梅姓柳秀才，招选一个，同生同死，可不美哉！（旦）怕等不得了。哎哟，哎哟！（贴）这病根儿怎攻[32]，心上医怎逢？（旦）春香，我亡后，你常向灵位前叫唤我一声儿。（贴）他一星星说向咱伤情重。（合前）（旦昏介）不好了，不好了，老爷奶奶快来！

【忆莺儿】（外、老旦上）鼓三冬，愁万重。冷雨幽窗灯不红。听侍儿传言女病凶。（贴泣介）我的小姐，小姐！（外、老旦同泣介）我的儿啊，你舍的命终，抛的我途穷。当初只望把爹娘送。（合）恨匆匆，萍踪浪影，风剪了玉芙蓉。（旦作醒介）（外）快苏醒！儿，爹在此。（旦作看外介）哎哟，爹爹扶我中堂去罢。（外）扶你也，儿。（扶介）

【尾声】（旦）怕树头树底不到的五更风[33]，和俺小坟边立断肠碑一统[34]。爹，今夜是中秋。（外）是中秋也，儿。（旦）禁了这一夜雨。（叹介）怎能勾月落重生灯再红！（并下）

（外）魂归冥漠魄归泉，朱　褒
（老）使汝悠悠十八年。曹　唐
（末）一叫一回肠一断，李　白
（合）如今重说恨绵绵。张　籍

注释

[1]颦有为颦，笑有为笑：当忧则忧，当喜则喜，意思是言行、情绪不能随便。

[2]长命灯：昼夜点燃的灯，以此祈求福寿。

[3]枕函：即枕匣，这里指枕头。

[4]冰蟾：月亮。

[5]在眉峰，心坎里别是一般疼痛：语本李清照词《一剪梅》："此情无计可消除。才下眉头，却上心头。"

[6]厮和哄：厮，相；和哄，欺骗、调弄。

[7]雾和烟两不玲珑：意思说春天不好。雾，烟，代表春天。

[8]侬：人，苏浙一带方言。

[9]蘸破：点破，照破。

[10]剪：比喻风吹落梧桐叶。

[11]楞生瘦骨加沉重：瘦骨峻嶒，病情更严重了。

[12]趱程期：赶路，赶时辰。

[13]软兀剌四梢难动：软兀剌，软绵绵地。兀剌，原为蒙古语，用在词尾，无意义。四梢，四肢。

[14]梦铳：睡梦。铳，瞌铳，苏浙方言，即瞌睡。

[15]不惺忪：神志不清爽。

[16]睡临侵：睡昏昏地。临侵，用在词尾，无意义，也写作淋浸。

[17]头梢：头。原指头发。

[18]乘龙：嫁个好女婿。

[19]阳神：生魂。

[20]风马：指悬在檐间的铁马。

[21]荡得个娇香种：好容易养了一个好女儿。

[22]高堂送：指给父母送终。

[23]月直年空：一作“年冲月空”，迷信的说法，冲、空都指大不利，这里指丽娘病危。或作“月值年灾”解，戏曲中熟语，意即某年或某月命定的灾厄，这里为协韵改了灾字。

[24]奔：这里指把遗体送走。

[25]旅榇：寄存外乡的棺木。

[26]是不是：无论如何，不管怎样。

[27]做不的病婵娟桂窟里长生：做不成带病的嫦娥住在月宫里长生不死。

[28]分（fèn）：应该。

[29]银蟾谩捣君臣药：谩，徒然。君臣药，药：中医配药，主治药品叫君，辅助药品叫臣。

[30]纸马重烧子母钱：纸马，一名甲马，纸上以彩色画神像，祭奠时用，用毕即焚化。子母钱，这里指纸钱。

[31]傥直那人知重：傥，即倘，也许；直，值，碰到；知重，知心，爱重。

[32]攻：医治。

[33]怕树头树底不到的五更风：怕满树的花朵，不待五更风的吹折，就已经落尽了。

[34]一统：一方，一块。

第四出 冥 判

（净扮判官，丑扮鬼持笔、簿上）

【那吒令】瞧了你润风风粉腮[1]，到花台、酒台？溜些些短钗[2]，过歌台、舞台？笑微微美怀，住秦台、楚台[3]？因甚的病患来？是谁家嫡支派？这颜色不像似在泉台[4]。（旦）女囚不曾过人家[5]，也不曾饮酒，是这般颜色。则为在南安府后花园梅树之下，梦见一秀才，折柳一枝，要奴题咏。留连婉转，甚是多情。梦醒来沉吟，题诗一首："他年若傍蟾宫客，不是梅边是柳边。"为此感伤，坏了一命。（净）谎也。世有一梦而亡之理？

【鹊踏枝】一溜溜女婴孩[6]，梦儿里能宁耐[7]！谁曾挂圆梦招牌[8]，谁和你拆字道白[9]？哈也么哈，那秀才何在？梦魂中曾见谁来？（旦）不曾见谁。则见朵花儿闪下来，好一惊。（净）唤取南安府后花园花神勘问。（丑叫介）（末扮花神上）"红雨数番春落魄[10]，山香一曲女消魂[11]。"老判大人请了。（举手介）（净）花神，这女鬼说是后花园一梦，为花飞惊闪而亡。可是？（末）是也。他与秀才梦的绵缠，偶尔落花惊醒。这女子慕色而亡。（净）敢便是你花神假充秀才，迷误人家女子？（末）你说俺着甚迷他来？（净）你说俺阴司里不知道呵！……这女囚慕色而亡，也贬在燕莺队里去罢。（末）禀老判，此女犯乃梦中之罪，如晓风残月。且他父亲为官清正，单生一女，可以耽饶。（净）父亲是何人？（旦）父亲杜宝知府，今升淮扬总制之职。（净）千金小姐哩。也罢，杜老先生分上，当奏过天庭，再行议处。（旦）就烦恩官替女犯查查，怎生有此伤感之事？（净）这事情注在断肠薄上。（旦）劳再查女犯的丈夫，还是姓柳姓梅？（净）取婚姻簿查来。（作背查介）是。有个柳梦梅，乃新科状元也。妻杜丽娘，前系幽欢，后成明配。相会在红梅观中。不可泄漏。（回介）有此人和你姻缘之分。我今放你出了枉死城，随风游戏，跟寻此人。（末）杜小姐，拜了老判。（旦叩头介）拜谢恩官，重生父母。

（末）醉斜乌帽发如丝，许　浑
（旦）尽日灵风不满旗。李商隐
（净）年年检点人间事，罗　邺
（合）为待萧何作判司。元　稹

注释

[1]润风风粉腮：娇嫩红润的脸色。

[2]溜些些短钗：短钗微斜。

[3]秦台、楚台：秦台，传说中秦国弄玉和爱人萧史同居的所在，见《列仙传》。楚台，即阳台，楚怀王与神女欢会的地方。

[4]泉台：黄泉，阴间。

[5]过人家：指出嫁。

[6]一溜溜：一点点大。

[7]能宁耐：这样有本事。

[8]挂圆梦招牌：指以解梦为职业。古人认为梦关乎人的吉凶祸福。

[9]拆字道白：即拆字，一作测字，把字拆开以占卜运气好坏的一种方法。

[10]落魄：潦倒、失意，这里指春残。

[11]山香一曲女消魂：山香，曲名。古代神话：西王母宴群仙，有舞者舞“山香”，曲未终，花纷纷落下。

第五本

第一出 拾画

【金珑璁】（生上）惊春谁似我？客途中都不问其他。风吹绽蒲桃褐[1]，雨淋殷杏子罗[2]。今日晴和，晒衾单兀自有残云涴[3]。“脉脉梨花春院香，一年愁事费商量。不知柳思能多少[4]？打叠腰肢斗沈郎[5]。”小生卧病梅花观中，喜得陈友知医，调理痊可。则这几日间春怀郁闷，何处忘忧？早是老姑姑到也[6]。

【一落索】（净上）无奈女冠何，识的书生破。知他何处梦儿多？每日价欠伸千个。秀才安稳[7]！（生）日来病患较些[8]，闷坐不过。偌大梅花观，少甚园亭消遣。（净）此后有花园一座，虽然亭榭荒芜，颇有闲花点缀。则留散闷，不许伤心。（生）怎的得伤心也！（净作叹介）是这般说。你自去游便了。从西廊转画墙而去，百步之外，便是篱门。三里之遥，都为池馆。你尽情玩赏，竟日消停，不索老身陪去也。“名园随客到，幽恨少人知。”（下）（生）既有后花园，就此迤逦而去[9]。（行介）这是西廊下了。（行介）好个葱翠的篱门，倒了半架。（叹介）（集唐）“凭阑仍是玉阑干王初，四面墙垣不忍看张隐。想得当时好风月韦庄，万条烟罩一时干[10]李山甫。”（到介）呀，偌大一个园子也。

【好事近】则见风月暗消磨，画墙西正南侧左。（跌介）苍苔滑擦，倚逗着断垣低垛，因何蝴蝶门儿落合[11]？原来以前游客颇盛，题名在竹林之上。客来过，年月偏多，刻画尽琅玕千个[12]。咳，早则是寒花绕砌，荒草成窠。怪哉，一个梅花观，女冠之流，怎起的这座大园子？好疑惑也。便是这湾流水呵！

【锦缠道】门儿锁，放着这武陵源一座。恁好处教颓堕！断烟中见水阁摧残，画船抛躲，冷秋千尚挂下裙拖。又不是曾经兵火，似这般狼籍呵，敢断肠人远、伤心事多？待不关情么，恰湖山石畔留着你打磨陀。好一座山子哩。（窥介）呀，就里一个小匣儿。待把左侧一峰靠着，看是何物？（作石倒介）呀，是个檀香匣儿。（开匣看画介）呀，一幅观世音喜相。善哉，善哉！待小生捧到书馆，顶礼供养，强如埋在此中。

【千秋岁】（捧匣回介）小嵯峨[13]，压的旃檀合[14]，便做了好相观音俏楼阁。片石峰前，那片石峰前，多则是飞来石[15]，三生因果。请将去炉烟上过[16]，头纳地，添灯火，照的他慈悲我[17]。俺这里尽情供养，他于意云何[18]？（到介）到了观中，且安置阁儿上，择日展礼。（净上）柳相公多早了！

【尾声】（生）姑姑，一生为客恨情多，过冷澹园林日午矬[19]。老姑姑，你道不许伤心，你为俺再寻一个定不伤心何处可。

（生）僻居虽爱近林泉，伍　乔
（净）早是伤春梦雨天。韦　庄
（生）何处邈将归画府？谭用之
（合）三峰花半碧堂悬。钱　起

注释

[1]蒲桃褐：印染着葡萄花样的粗布衣服。

[2]雨淋殷杏子罗：红罗着水而颜色消褪，浓淡不匀。殷，红色。

[3]残云涴：指路途遇雨，衾被还有湿渍。

[4]柳思；春思。

[5]打叠腰肢斗沈郎：意思是说自己消瘦。沈郎，南朝沈约写自己腰瘦，后来即以沈腰或沈郎腰指腰瘦。这里又以柳梦梅的姓柳与“柳腰”相联系。

[6]早是：幸是。

[7]安稳：犹如说“你好”。

[8]较：病好一些。

[9]迤逦：形容路径蜿蜒，这里可作慢慢解。

[10]万条烟罩：形容柳条繁多。

[11]蝴蝶门儿落合：蝴蝶门，一种双扇门的样式；落合，闩着。

[12]琅玕：玉名，用作竹的代称。

[13]嵯峨：形容山势险峻，这里指假山。下文楼阁也指假山。

[14]旃檀合：旃檀，香木名，梵语旃檀那的省译，是檀香的原料。合，同盒。

[15]飞来石：杭州西湖灵隐有飞来峰，有人说这是中天竺国（在印度）灵鹫山的小岭，不知哪那年飞到这里来的，山因此而得名。这里也是指假山。

[16]请将去炉烟上过：指把画像迎请去，薰了香，然后叩头礼拜。

[17]头纳地，添灯火，照的他慈悲我：意思是说，叩头点灯照亮菩萨画像，以虔敬的心使得菩萨保佑我。

[18]于意云何：以为何如，认为怎么样，佛经里常见的句子。

[19]矬：指日斜。

第二出 玩 真

（生上）“芭蕉叶上雨难留，芍药梢头风欲收。画意无明偏着眼，春光有路暗抬头。”小生客中孤闷，闲游后园。湖山之下，拾得一轴小画，似是观音大士，宝匣庄严。风雨淹旬，未能展视。且喜今日晴和，瞻礼一会。（开匣，展画介）

【黄莺儿】秋影挂银河，展天身，自在波[1]。诸般好相能停妥[2]。他真身在补陀[3]，咱海南人遇他。（想介）甚威光不上莲花座？再延俄，怎湘裙直下一对小凌波[4]？是观音，怎一对小脚儿？待俺端详一会。

【二郎神慢】些儿个，画图中影儿则度[5]。着了，敢谁书馆中吊下幅小嫦娥，画的这傅停倭妥[6]。是嫦娥，一发该顶戴了。问嫦娥折桂人有我？可是嫦娥，怎影儿外没半朵祥云托？树皴儿又不似桂丛花琐[7]？不是观音，又不是嫦娥，人间那得有此？成惊愕，似曾相识，向俺心头摸。待俺瞧，是画工临的，还是美人自手描的？

【莺啼序】问丹青何处娇娥，片月影光生毫末[8]？似恁般一个人儿，早见了百花低躲。总天然意态难模，谁近得把春云淡破？想来画工怎能到此！多敢他自己能描会脱[9]。且住，细观他帧首之上，小字数行。（看介）呀，原来绝句一首。（念介）“近睹分明似俨然，远观自在若飞仙。他年得傍蟾宫客，不在梅边在柳边。”呀，此乃人间女子行乐图也。何言“不在梅边在柳边”？奇哉怪事哩！

【集贤宾】望关山梅岭天一抹，怎知俺柳梦梅过？得傍蟾宫知怎么？待喜呵，端详停和[10]，俺姓名儿直么费嫦娥定夺？打磨诃[11]，敢则是梦魂中真个。好不回盼小生！

【黄莺儿】空影落纤娥，动春蕉，散绮罗。春心只在眉间锁，春山翠拖[12]，春烟淡和。相看四目谁轻可[13]！恁横波，来回顾影不住的眼儿睃。却怎半枝青梅在手，活似提掇小生一般？

【啼莺序】他青梅在手诗细哦，逗春心一点蹉跎。小生待画饼充饥[14]，小姐似望梅止渴[15]。小姐，小姐，未曾开半点幺荷[16]，含笑处朱唇淡抹，韵情多。如愁欲语，只少口气儿呵[17]。小娘子画似崔徽，诗如苏蕙[18]，行书逼真卫夫人。小子虽则典雅，怎到得这小娘子[19]！蓦地相逢，不免步韵一首[20]。（题介）"丹青妙处却天然，不是天仙即地仙。欲傍蟾宫人近远，恰些春在柳梅边。"

【簇御林】他能绰斡[21]，会写作。秀入江山人唱和。待小生很很叫他几声："美人，美人！姐姐，姐姐！"向真真啼血你知么？叫的你喷嚏似天花唾。动凌波，盈盈欲下——不见影儿那。咳，俺孤单在此，少不得将小娘子画像，早晚玩之、拜之，叫之、赞之。

【尾声】拾的个人儿先庆贺，敢柳和梅有些瓜葛[22]？小姐小姐，则被你有影无形看杀我。

不须一向恨丹青，白居易
堪把长悬在户庭。伍　乔
惆怅题诗柳中隐，司空图
添成春醉转难醒。章　碣

注释

[1]自在波：自在，观自在菩萨，即观音。波，同呵、啊。

[2]诸般好相：佛家语，应身佛肉体上有三十二妙相，如手指纤长、身金色等等。

[3]补陀：即普陀。一名补陀落迦，舟山群岛所属小岛。佛家传说这里是观世音菩萨说法的圣地。

[4]小凌波：指女性的小脚。

[5]度(duó)：猜度。

[6]倭妥：即委佗，美好。

[7]花琐：细碎的花朵，指桂花。

[8]毫末：笔端。

[9]脱：脱稿、描画的意思。

[10]停和：消停，这里的意思是细看一会儿。

[11]打磨诃：即打磨陀，这里是徘徊、思量的意思。

[12]春山：指眉。

[13]轻可：轻易，等闲。

[14]画饼充饥：原喻有名无实，这里是聊以自慰之意。

[15]望梅上渴：比喻可望不可即。

[16]幺荷：荷花蕾，形容嘴唇。幺，小。

[17]呵：呵气，动词。

[18]苏蕙：前秦窦滔妻。窦滔做秦州刺史，因事被流放，苏蕙织锦为回文，凡八百四十字。纵横反复，皆成章句，名《璇玑图》，寄给丈夫。

[19]到得：及得，比得上。

[20]步韵：依照别人诗所用的韵作诗相和。

[21]绰斡：这里指作画。

[22]瓜葛：瓜、葛都有藤蔓，用来喻亲戚或一般的关联。

第三出 魂 游

【水红花】（魂旦作鬼声，掩袖上）则下得望乡台如梦俏魂灵，夜荧荧、墓门人静。（内犬吠，旦惊介）原来是赚花阴小犬吠春星[1]。冷冥冥，梨花春影。呀，转过牡丹亭、芍药阑，都荒废尽。爹娘去了三年也。（泣介）伤感煞断垣荒径。望中何处也？鬼灯青。（听介）兀的有人声也啰[2]。（添字昭君怨）“昔日千金小姐，今日水流花谢。这淹淹惜惜杜陵花[3]，太亏他。生性独行无那[4]，此夜星前一个。生生死死为情多。奈情何！”奴家杜丽娘女魂是也。只为痴情慕色，一梦而亡。凑的十地阎君奉旨裁革[5]，无人发遣，女监三年。喜遇老判，哀怜放假。趁此月明风细，随喜一番。呀，这是书斋后园，怎做了梅花庵观？好伤感人也。

【小桃红】咱一似断肠人和梦醉初醒。谁偿咱残生命也。虽则鬼丛中姊妹不同行，窣地的把罗衣整[6]。这影随形，风沉露，云暗斗，月勾星[7]，都是我魂游境也。到的这花影初更，（内作丁冬声，旦惊介）一霎价心儿瘆[8]，原来是弄风铃台殿冬丁。好一阵香也。

【下山虎】呀，那边厢有沉吟叫唤之声，听怎来？（内叫介）俺的姐姐呵！俺的美人呵！（旦惊介）谁叫谁也？再听。（内又叫介）（旦叹介）

【醉归迟】生和死，孤寒命。有情人叫不出情人应。为什么不唱出你可人名姓[9]？似俺孤魂独趁，待谁来叫唤俺一声。不分明，无倒断[10]，再消停。（内又叫介）（旦）咳，敢边厢什么书生，睡梦里语言胡哩[11]？

【黑蟆令】不由俺无情有情，凑着叫的人三声两声，冷惺忪红泪飘零。呀，怕不是梦人儿梅卿柳卿？俺记着这花亭水亭，趁的这风清月清。则这鬼宿前程，盼得上三星四星[12]？待即行寻趁，奈斗转参横[13]，不敢久停呵！

注释

[1]赚花阴：花影动，误以为人来。赚，骗。

[2]也啰：感叹词。

[3]淹淹惜惜杜陵花：淹淹惜惜，形容多情。杜陵花，喻杜家的女儿，即杜丽娘。

[4]无那：无奈。

[5]凑的：碰着。

[6]窣地的把罗衣整：整理拖在地上的罗衣。窣地，拖地，形容衣服很长。

[7]月勾星：即辰钩月，月蚀。辰星一名钩星，即水星。

[8]瘆(shèn)：惊恐。

[9]可人：可爱的人。

[10]倒断：了结，休止。

[11]胡哩：胡言乱语。

[12]则这鬼宿前程，盼得上三星、四星：做了鬼，姻缘前途还能有几分拿得准呢？

[13]斗转参横：指夜深。斗、参，星宿名，从它们的运行可以看出大约是什么时候。

第四出 幽 媾

【夜行船】（生上）瞥下天仙何处也？影空濛似月笼沙。有恨徘徊，无言窨约。早是夕阳西下。“一片红云下太清[1]，如花巧笑玉娉婷。凭谁画出生香面？对俺偏含不语情。”小生自遇春容，日夜想念。这更兰时节，破些工夫，吟其珠玉[2]，玩其精神。倘然梦里相亲，也当春风一度。（展画玩介）呀，你看美人呵，神含欲语，眼注微波。真乃“落霞与孤鹜齐飞，秋水共长天一色[3]”。

【香遍满】晚风吹下，武陵溪边一缕霞，出落个人儿风韵杀。净无瑕，明窗新绛纱。丹青小画，又把一幅肝肠挂。小姐小姐，则被你想杀俺也。

【懒画眉】轻轻怯怯一个女娇娃，楚楚臻臻像个宰相衙[4]。想他春心无那对菱花，含情自把春容画，可想到有个拾翠人儿也逗着他？

【二犯梧桐树】他飞来似月华，俺拾的愁天大。常时夜夜对月而眠，这几夜呵，幽佳，婵娟隐映的光辉杀。教俺迷留没乱的心嘈杂[5]，无夜无明怏着他。若不为擎奇怕涴的丹青亚[6]，待抱着你影儿横榻。想来小生定是有缘也。再将他诗句朗诵一番。（念诗介）

【浣纱溪】拈诗话，对会家[7]。柳和梅有分儿些[8]。他春心迸出湖山罅，飞上烟绡萼绿华[9]。则是礼拜他便了。（拈香拜介）傒幸杀[10]，对他脸晕眉痕心上掐，有情人不在天涯。小生客居，怎勾姐姐风月中片时相会也。

【刘泼帽】恨单条不惹的双魂化[11]，做个画屏中倚玉蒹葭[12]。小姐呵，你耳朵儿云鬓月侵芽[13]，可知他一些些都听的俺伤情话？

【秋夜月】堪笑咱，说的来如戏耍。他海天秋月云端挂，烟空翠影遥山抹。只许他伴人清暇，怎教人佻达[14]。

【东瓯令】俺如念咒，似说法。石也要点头[15]，天雨花[16]。怎虔诚不降的仙娥下？是不肯轻行踏。（内作风起，生按住画介）待留仙怕杀风儿刮，粘嵌着锦边牙[17]。怕刮损他，再寻个高手临他一幅儿。

【金莲子】闲啧牙[18]，怎能勾他威光水月生临榻[19]？怕有处相逢他自家，则问他许多情，与春风画意再无差。再把灯剔起细看他一会。（照介）。

【隔尾】敢人世上似这天真多则假[20]。（内作风吹灯介）（生）好一阵冷风袭人也。险些儿误丹青风影落灯花。罢了，则索睡掩纱窗去梦他。（打睡介）（魂旦上）“泉下长眠梦不成。一生余得许多情。魂随月下丹青引，人在风前叹息声。”妾身杜丽娘鬼魂是也。为花园一梦，想念而终。当时自画春容，埋于太湖石下。题有“他年得傍蟾宫客，不在梅边在柳边”。谁想魂游观中几晚，听见东房之内，一个书生高声低叫：“俺的姐姐，俺的美人。”那声音哀楚，动俺心魂。悄然蓦入他房中[21]，则见高挂起一轴小画。细玩之，便是奴家遗下春容。后面和诗一首，观其名字，则岭南柳梦梅也。梅边柳边，岂非前定乎！因而告过了冥府判君，趁此良宵，完其前梦。想起来好苦也。

【朝天懒】怕的是粉冷香销泣绛纱，又到的高唐馆玩月华。猛回头羞飒[22]髻儿鬈[23]，自擎拿。呀，前面是他房头了。怕桃源

路径行来诧，再得俄旋试认他。（生睡中念诗介）“他年若傍蟾宫客，不在梅边在柳边。”我的姐姐啊。（旦）（听打悲介）

【前腔】是他叫唤的伤情咱泪雨麻，把我残诗句没争差。难道还未睡呵？（瞧介）（生又叫介）（旦）他原来睡屏中作念猛嗟牙[24]。省喧哗，我待敲弹翠竹窗栊下。（生作惊醒，叫“姐姐”介）（旦悲介）待展香魂去近他。（生）呀，户外敲竹之声，是风是人？（旦）有人。（生）这咱时节有人[25]，敢是老姑姑送茶来？免劳了。（旦）不是。（生）敢是游方的小姑姑么？（旦）不是。（生）好怪，好怪，又不是小姑姑。再有谁？待我启门而看。（生开门看介）

【玩仙灯】呀，何处一娇娃，艳非常使人惊诧。（旦作笑闪入）（生急掩门）（旦敛衽整容见介）秀才万福。（生）小娘子到来，敢问尊前何处，因何夤夜至此[26]？（旦）秀才，你猜来。

【红衲袄】（生）莫不是莽张骞犯了你星汉槎[27]，莫不是小梁清夜走天曹罚[28]？（旦）这都是天上仙人，怎得到此。（生）是人家彩凤暗随鸦[29]？（旦摇头介）（生）敢甚处里绿杨曾系马[30]？（旦）不曾一面。（生）若不是认陶潜眼挫的花[31]，敢则是走临邛道数儿差[32]？（旦）非差。（生）想是求灯的？可是你夜行无烛也[33]，因此上待要红袖分灯向碧纱？

【前腔】（旦）俺不为度仙香空散花[34]，也不为读书灯闲濡蜡。俺不似赵飞卿旧有瑕[35]，也不似卓文君新守寡。秀才呵，你也曾随蝶梦迷花下[36]。（生想介）是当初曾梦来。（旦）俺因此上弄莺簧赴柳衙[37]。若问俺妆台何处也，不远哩，刚则在宋玉东邻第几家。（生作想介）是了。曾后花园转西，夕阳时节，见小娘子走动哩。（旦）便是了。（生）家下有谁？

【宜春令】（旦）斜阳外，芳草涯，再无人有伶仃的爹妈。奴年二八，没包弹风藏叶里花[38]。为春归惹动嗟呀，瞥见你风神俊雅。无他，待和你翦烛临风，西窗闲话。（生背介）奇哉，奇哉，人间有此艳色！夜半无故而遇明月之珠，怎生发付！

【前腔】他惊人艳，绝世佳。闪一笑风流银蜡[39]。月明如乍，问今夕何年星汉槎？金钗客寒夜来家，玉天仙人间下榻。（背介）知他，知他是甚宅眷的孩儿，这迎门调法[40]？待小生再问他。（回介）小娘子夤夜下顾小生，敢是梦也？（旦笑介）不是梦，当真哩。还怕秀才未肯容纳。（生）则怕未真。果然美人见爱，小生喜出望外。何敢却乎？（旦）这等真个盼着你了。

【耍鲍老】幽谷寒涯，你为俺催花连夜发。俺全然未嫁，你个中知察，拘惜的好人家。牡丹亭，娇恰恰；湖山畔，羞答答；读书窗，淅喇喇[41]。良夜省陪茶，清风明月知无价。

【滴滴金】（生）俺惊魂化，睡醒时凉月些些。陡地荣华，敢则是梦中巫峡[42]？亏杀你走花阴不害些儿怕，点苍苔不溜些儿滑，背萱亲不受些儿吓，认书生不着些儿差。你看斗儿斜，花儿亚，如此夜深花睡罢。笑咖咖，吟哈哈，风月无加。把他艳软香娇做意儿耍，下的亏他[43]？便亏他则半霎。（旦）妾有一言相恳，望郎恕罪。（生笑介）贤卿有话，但说无妨。（旦）妾千金之躯，一旦付与郎矣，勿负奴心。每夜得共枕席，平生之愿足矣。（生笑介）贤卿有心恋于小生，小生岂敢忘于贤卿乎？（旦）还有一言。未至鸡鸣，放奴回去。秀才休送，以避晓风。（生）这都领命。只问姐姐贵姓芳名？

【意不尽】（旦叹介）少不得花有根元玉有芽[44]，待说时惹的风声大。（生）以后准望贤卿逐夜而来。（旦）秀才，且和

俺点勘春风**这**第一花。

（生）**浩态狂香昔未逢，**韩　愈
（旦）**月斜楼上五更钟。**李商隐
（旦）**朝云夜入无行处，**李　白
（生）**神女知来第几峰？**张子容

注释

[1]太清：天。

[2]珠玉：喻诗文佳作。

[3]落霞与孤鹜齐飞，秋水共长天一色：语出唐王勃《滕王阁序》。

[4]宰相衙：这里指宰相的小姐。

[5]迷留没乱：心绪紊乱。

[6]擎奇：即奇擎，奇无义。擎，举。

[7]拈诗话，对会家：意思是说，杜丽娘的诗是为他这个知心人写的。

[8]有分儿些：有些缘分。

[9]飞上烟绡萼绿华：萼绿华，神话中女仙名。这句的意思是好像仙女飞上绢幅，变成美丽的画像。

[10]傒幸：烦恼，疑惑。

[11]单条：狭长的独幅字画。

[12]做个画屏中倚玉蒹葭：蒹葭，荻，贱物，这里是柳梦梅自谦的比喻。全句意思说，恨不得自己也进入画中，变成她的陪衬。

[13]耳朵儿云鬓月侵芽：芽，指月牙，新月；侵，遮掩。这里以云遮月比喻发掩耳。

[14]佻达：戏谑。

[15]石也要点头：佛家传说，梁高僧竺道生在苏州虎丘讲法，石皆点头。

[16]天雨花：佛家传说，梁高僧云光法师在南京雨花台讲经，天下落下花雨。

[17]锦边牙：裱好的画幅上端的部位，供张挂用。

[18]闲啧牙：说空话，多嘴。

[19]威光水月生临榻：威光水月，指水月观音，这里指画中美人。生临榻，活灵活现地来到床上。

[20]似这天真多则假：天真，天仙。多则假，多半是假的。

[21]蓦：迈。

[22]飒：象声词。

[23]鬖：这里是说发髻歪斜。

[24]睡屏中作念猛嗟牙：睡屏中，犹言床上，引申作睡梦中。作念，指想念。嗟牙，即嗟讶，嗟叹。

[25]这咱时节：这会儿、这般时候。

[26]夤夜：深夜。

[27]张骞犯了你星汉槎：神话传说，汉张骞乘水上浮木（槎）到银河边牵牛、织女那里。

[28]梁清：神话中女仙名，可能指织女的侍儿梁玉清，相传她与太白星逃到下界。

[29]彩凤暗随鸦：宋杜大中是军人出身，他的爱妾能词，写词抱怨自己是彩凤随鸦，没嫁到好丈夫。

[30]绿杨曾系马：曾下马去看过她。

[31]认陶潜眼挫的花：陶潜，晋代诗人，《桃花源记》的作者。眼挫的花，眼花错看。这里把陶渊当作入天台逢仙女的刘晨、阮肇一流人物，意思是说找情郎看错了人。

[32]走临邛道数儿差：走临邛，指私奔。卓文君是四川临邛人，寡居在家，与司马相如私奔。

[33]夜行无烛：语出《礼•内则》："女子出门……夜行以烛，无烛则止。"

[34]度仙香空散花：佛家传说，文殊到维摩诘那里问病，天女散花，花飞到菩萨身上即落下，散在大弟子身上的却粘着不落。天女说，这是因为大弟子结习还没有尽。

[35]赵飞卿旧有瑕：赵飞卿，或指汉成帝的皇后赵飞燕，相传她贫贱时曾和射鸟者私通。

[36]蝶梦：指梦，语出《庄子•齐物论》："昔者庄周梦为胡蝶，栩栩然胡蝶也。"

[37]弄莺簧赴柳衙：簧，乐器名，用簧声来形容莺鸣。柳衙，柳成行；衙，排衙，原指长官排列仪仗，接受属员的参谒；这里指柳梦梅的住处。

[38]没包弹：无可指摘，无可批评。

[39]银蜡：蜡烛。

[40]调法：耍花样。

[41]淅喇喇：形容风吹窗纸声。

[42]巫峡：这里实指巫山，喻男女欢会。

[43]下的：忍得。

[44]花有根元玉有芽：有根芽，有来历、有出处的意思。

第五出 欢 挠

【捣练子】（生上）听漏下半更多，月影向中那。恁时节夜香烧罢么？“一点猩红一点金，十个春纤十个针。只因世上美人面，改尽人间君子心。”俺柳梦梅是个读书君子，一味志诚。止因北上南安，凑着东邻西子。嫣然一笑，遂成暮雨之来；未是五更，便逐晓风而去。今宵有约，未知迟早。正是：“金莲若肯移三寸[1]，银烛先教刻五分[2]。”则一件，姐姐若到，要精神对付他。偷盹一会，有何不可。（睡介）

【称人心】（魂旦上）冥途挣挫[3]，要死却心儿无那。也则为俺那人儿忒可，教他闷房头守着闲灯火。（入门介）呀，他端然睡瞌，恁春寒也不把绣衾来摸。多应他祗候着我[4]。待叫醒他。秀才，秀才！（生醒介）姐姐，失敬也。（起揖介）（生）待整衣罗，远远相迎个。这二更天风露多，还则怕夜深花睡么？（旦）秀才，俺那里长夜好难过，缱着你无眠清坐。（生）姐姐，你来的脚踪儿恁轻，是怎的？（集唐）“（旦）自然无迹又无尘朱庆余，（生）白日寻思夜梦频令狐楚。（旦）行到窗前知未寝无名氏，（生）一心惟待月夫人皮日休。”姐姐，今夜来的迟些。

【绣带儿】（旦）镇消停，不是俺闲情忒慢俄。那些儿忘却俺欢哥[5]。夜香残，回避了尊亲。绣床偎收拾起生活[6]，停脱[7]。顺风儿斜将金佩拖，紧摘离百忙的淡妆明抹[8]。（生）费你高情，则良夜无酒奈何？（旦）都忘了。俺携酒一壶，花果二色，在楯栏之上，取来消遣。（旦取酒、果、花上）（生）生受了。是甚果？（旦）青梅数粒。（生）这花？（旦）美人蕉。（生）梅子酸似俺秀才，蕉花红似俺姐姐。串饮一杯。（共杯饮介）

【白练序】（旦）金荷[9]、斟香糯[10]。（生）你酝酿春心玉液波。拚微酡，东风外翠香红酦[11]。（旦）也摘不下奇花果，这一点蕉花和梅豆呵，君知么，爱的人全风韵，花有根科[12]。

【醉太平】（生）细哦，这子儿花朵，似美人憔悴，酸子情多。喜蕉心暗展，一夜梅犀点污[13]。如何？酒潮微晕笑生涡。待噷着脸恣情的呜嘬[14]，些儿个，翠偃了情波，润红蕉点，香生梅唾。

【白练序】（旦）活泼、死腾那，这是第一所人间风月窝。昨宵个微芒暗影轻罗，把势儿忒显豁[15]。为什么人到幽期话转多？（生）好睡也。（旦）好月也。消停坐，不妒色嫦娥，和俺人三个。

注：杜丽娘起死回生后，与柳梦梅结为夫妻。梦梅金榜题名，考取状元，双喜临门。

注释

[1]金莲：三寸金莲，形容女性的脚小。

[2]银烛先教刻五分：南朝梁竟陵王萧子良与友人夜集，刻烛为诗。做四韵诗刻一寸。

[3]挣挫：挣扎。

[4]祗候：这里用作动词，等候，

[5]欢哥：对情郎的昵称。

[6]生活：指针线活儿。

[7]停脱：停当，完毕。

[8]摘离：离开，脱身。

[9]荷：杯的代称，古代有荷叶杯。

[10]糯：指糯米做的酒。

[11]酘：以酒为原料再加蒸制而成的烈性酒。这里是形容花很红，再以花红喻酒醉。

[12]根科：根株，作根芽解。

[13]梅犀点污：隐喻欢会。梅犀，梅子。

[14]待嗽着脸恣情的呜嘬：尽情地吻。

[15]把势儿：指欢会的姿态。

Theory on Literary Translation of the Chinese School

The theory on literary translation of the Chinese school owes its origin to traditional Chinese culture, including the Confucian and the Taoist school of thought respectively represented by *Thus Spoke the Master* and *Laws Divine and Human.*

It is said in the first chapter of *Laws Divine and Human* that truth can be known, but it may not be the truth you know, and that things may be named, but names are not the things. When applied to literary translation, this may mean that the theory on literary translation can be known, but it may not the unproven theory on the one hand, nor the scientific theory on the other, for neither literary translation nor its theory is science. As the names are not equal to the things, the translation cannot be equal to the original. As there is more difference than equivalence between the Chinese and the English language, the principle of equivalence can not be applied to the translation between them as between two occidental languages.

It is said in the last chapter of *Laws Divine and Human* that truthful words may not be beautiful and beautiful words may not be truthful. That is to say, there is contradiction between truth and beauty or between equivalence and excellence. A translation where equivalents are used may be called a faithful or truthful translation. When no equivalent can be found between two languages, the translator should make use of the best expressions or excellent expressions of the target language. That may be called theory of excellence.

In *Thus Spoke the Master*, Confucius said, "At seventy, I can do what I will without going beyond what is right." Professor Zhu Guangqian said that this has shown the mature state of an artist. I think it may also show the mature state of a literary translator. The literal translator has used the equivalents without going beyond the original in sound; the liberal translator has described the image without going beyond the original in sense; the literary translator has described the scene without going beyond reality. Not to go beyond the original is to be truthful or faithful, and the translator has reached the ordinary level of translation. To do what one will without going beyond the original is not only to be faithful but also to make his translation beautiful, in that case the translator has attained a higher level. To excel the original without going beyond the reality it describes is to attain the highest level.

What is literary translation? It is an art of solving the contradiction between faithfulness (or truth) and beauty. How to solve it? There are three methods, namely, equalization, generalization and particularization. When there is little or no contradition between truth and beauty, equalization or equivalents may be used. When there is contradction between them, generalization may be used to make the meaning clear, and particularization to make a deeper impression.

Confucius said in *Thus Spoke the Master* that it would be good to be understandable, better to be enjoyable and best to be delectable or delightful. When applied to literary translation, this principle means that an understandable translation is good, an enjoyable one is better and a delightful one is best. The ontology or theory of contradition between truth and beauty, the methodology or theory of equalization, generalization and particularization, and the teleology or theory of the understandable, the enjoyable and the delectable, all owe their origin to the Confucian and Taoist schools of thoughts.

But Confucius said less about what delight is and more about how to be delightful. In the beginning of *Thus Spoke the Master* he said it is delightful to acquire knowledge and put it into practice; In Chapter Six he told us how Yan Hui could find delight in reading though living in a humble lane with only a handful of rice to eat and a gourdful of water to drink; In Chapter Eleven, Zeng Xi told us his delight in an spring excursion. From these examples we can see Confucius' theory on delight or teleology, and his theory on practice or methodology. His theory is not scientific but artistic. Since literary translation is an art but not a branch of science, his theory can not only be applied to the practice but also to the theory of literary translation. As his theory has stood the test of time, it is as durable as scientific theories. A theorist on science who studies truth and the truthful should not go beyond what is truthful. A theorist on art or an artist who studies beauty and the beautiful may go beyond what is truthful and faithful.

The contradiction between truth and beauty in Chinese theory on literary translation has developed into a contradiction between equivalence and excellence. As Keats said, "Beauty is truth, truth beauty," we may even say beauty is a virtue, a kind of excellence. When we cannot find the equivalent, we may resort to generalization or particularization.

In short, literary translation is an art to create the beautiful.

This is the epistemology of the Chinese school. The contradition between truth and beauty or between equivalence and excellence is its ontology; the theory on equalization, generalization and particularization is its triple methodology; and the theory of the understandable, the enjoyable and the delectable or delightful is its triple teleology.

Xu Yuanchong
Oct. 2011

代后记：中国学派的文学翻译理论

中国学派的文学翻译理论源自中国的传统文化，主要包括儒家思想和道家思想，儒家思想的代表著作是《论语》，道家思想的代表著作是《老子道德经》。

《老子道德经》第一章开始就说：“道可道，非常道；名可名，非常名。”联系到翻译理论上来，就是说：翻译理论是可以知道的，是可以说得出来的，但不是只说得出来而经不起实践检验的空头理论，这就是中国学派翻译理论中的实践论。其次，文学翻译理论不能算科学理论（自然科学），与其说是社会科学理论，不如说是人文学科或艺术理论，这就是文学翻译的艺术论，也可以说是相对论。后六个字“名可名，非常名”应用到文学翻译理论上来，可以有两层意思：第一层是原文的文字是描写现实的，但并不等于现实，文字和现实之间还有距离，还有矛盾；第二层意思是译文和原文之间也有距离，也有矛盾，译文和原文所描写的现实之间，自然还有距离，还有矛盾。译文应该发挥译语优势，运用最好的译语表达方式，来和原文展开竞赛，使译文和现实的距离或矛盾小于原文和现实之间的矛盾，那就是超越原文了。这就是文学翻译理论中的优势论或优化论，超越论或竞赛论。文学翻译理论应该解决的不只是译文和原文在文字方面的矛盾，还要解决译文和原文所反映的现实之间的矛盾，这是文学翻译的本体论。

一般翻译只要解决“真”或“信”或“似”的问题，文学翻译却要解决“真”或“信”和“美”之间的矛盾。原文反映的现实不只是言内之意，还有言外之意。中国的文学语言往往有言外之意，甚至还有言外之情。文学翻译理论也要解决译文和原文的言外之意、言外之情的矛盾。

《论语》说："知之者不如好之者，好之者不如乐之者。"知之，好之，乐之，这"三之论"是对艺术论的进一步说明。艺术论第一条原则要求译文忠实于原文所反映的现实，求的是真，可以使人知之；第二条原则要求用"三化"法来优化译文，求的是美，可以使人好之；第三条原则要求用"三美"来优化译文，尤其是译诗词，求的是意美、音美和形美，可以使人乐之。如果"不逾矩"的等化译文能使人知之（理解），那就达到了文学翻译的低标准，如从心所欲而不逾矩的浅化或深化的译文既能使人知之，又能使人好之（喜欢），那就达到了中标准；如果从心所欲的译文不但能使人知之，好之，还能使人乐之（愉快），那才达到了文学翻译的高标准。这也是中国译者对世界译论作出的贡献。

翻译艺术的规律是从心所欲而不逾矩。"矩"就是规矩，规律。但艺术规律却可以依人的主观意志而转移，是因为得到承认才算正确的。所以贝多芬说：为了更美，没有什么清规戒律不可打破。他所说的戒律不是科学规律，而是艺术规律。不能用科学规律来评论文学翻译。

孔子不大谈"什么是"(What?)而多谈"怎么做"(How?)。这是中国传统的方法论，比西方流传更久，影响更广，作用更大，并且经过了两三千年实践的考验。《论语》第一章中说："学而时习之，不亦说（悦，乐）乎！""学"是取得知识，"习"是实践。孔子只说学习实践可以得到乐趣，却不说什么是"乐"。这就是孔子的方法论，是中国文学翻译理论的依据。

总而言之，中国学派的文学翻译理论是研究老子提出的

"信"（似）"美"（优）矛盾的艺术（本体论），但"信"不限原文，还指原文所反映的现实，这是认识论，"信"由严复提出的"信达雅"发展到鲁迅提出"信顺"的直译，再发展到陈源的"三似"（形似，意似，神似），直到傅雷的"重神似不重形似"，这已经接近"美"了。"美"发展到鲁迅的"三美"（意美，音美，形美），再发展到林语堂提出的"忠实，通顺，美"，转化为朱生豪"传达原作意趣"的意译，直到茅盾提出的"美的享受"。孔子提出的"从心所欲"发展到郭沫若提出的创译论（好的翻译等于创作），以及钱钟书说的译文可以胜过原作的"化境"说，再发展到优化论，超越论，"三化"（等化，浅化，深化）方法论。孔子提出的"不逾矩"和老子说的"信言不美，美言不信"有同有异。老子"信美"并重，孔子"从心所欲"重于"不逾矩"，发展为朱光潜的"艺术论"，包括郭沫若说的"在信达之外，愈雅愈好。所谓'雅'不是高深或讲修饰，而是文学价值或艺术价值比较高。"直到茅盾说的："必须把文学翻译工作提高到艺术创造的水平。"孔子的"乐之"发展为胡适之的"愉快"说（翻译要使读者读得愉快），再发展到"三之"（知之，好之，乐之）目的论。这就是中国学派的文学翻译理论发展为"美化之艺术"（"三美"，"三化"，"三之"的艺术）的概况。

许渊冲

2011年10月

图书在版编目（CIP）数据

牡丹亭: 汉英对照 / 许渊冲译. — 北京: 五洲传播出版社,
2018.1（2021.8重印）
（许译中国经典诗文集）
ISBN 978-7-5085-3896-9

Ⅰ. ①牡… Ⅱ. ①许… Ⅲ. ①汉语—英语—对照读物 ②传奇剧（戏曲）—剧本—中国—明代 Ⅳ. ①H319.4：I

中国版本图书馆CIP数据核字(2017)第323691号

牡丹亭

译　　者：许渊冲　许　明
策划编辑：荆孝敏
责任编辑：王　峰
中文编辑：张　梅
英文编辑：马培武　鲁大东
装帧设计：北京正视文化艺术有限责任公司
出版发行：五洲传播出版社
地　　址：北京市海淀区北三环中路31号生产力大楼B座6层
邮　　编：100088
电　　话：010—82005927，010-82007837
网　　址：http://www.cicc.org.cn　http://www.thatsbooks.com
印　　刷：北京市房山腾龙印刷厂
版　　次：2012年1月第1版　2021年8月第2版第3次印刷
开　　本：140mm × 210mm　1/32
印　　张：8.25
字　　数：240千字
书　　号：ISBN 978-7-5085-3896-9
定　　价：79.00元